# REFLECTIONS

ON

# THE PRESENT STATE

OF

# BRITISH INDIA

# REFLECTIONS

ON

# THE PRESENT STATE

OF

# BRITISH INDIA.

HENRY DUNDAS ROBERTSON,
GAVIN YOUNG

GYAN

*Published by*

Gyan Publishing House
5, Ansari Road
Daryaganj, New Delhi-110002
Phone: 011-47034999, 9811692060
E-mail: books@gyanbooks.com

*Distribution Network*
gyanbooks.com
India, USA, Canada, UK, Australia



ISBN: 978-81-212-7051-9 (PB)
First Published, 1829

2nd Impression 2024

*Printed at:* Gyan Press, Delhi.



**REFLECTIONS ON THE PRESENT STATE OF BRITISH INDIA**
Author: HENRY DUNDAS ROBERTSON, GAVIN YOUNG

# REFLECTIONS

ON

# THE PRESENT STATE

OF

# BRITISH INDIA.

# REFLECTIONS

ON

# THE PRESENT STATE

OF

# BRITISH INDIA.

---

" Ad illa mihi pro se quisque acriter intendat animum, quæ vitæ, qui mores fuerunt—per quos viros, quibusque artibus, domi militiæque, et partum et auctum imperium sit." Liv. *Præf.*

" Primò pecuniæ, dein imperii cupido crevit, et quasi materies omnium malorum fuere. Namque avaritia fidem, probitatem, ceterasque artes bonas subvertit; pro his superbiam, crudelitatem, Deos negligere, omnia venalia habere, edocuit; ambitio multos mortales falsos fieri subegit; aliud clausum in pectore, aliud promptum in linguâ habere; amicitias inimicitiasque non ex re, sed ex commodo, æstumare; magisque vultum quam ingenium, bonum habere." Sall.

" Cum per se res mutentur in deterius si consilio in melius non mutentur, quis finis erit mali?" Lord Bacon.

---

LONDON:

HURST, CHANCE, AND CO., ST. PAUL'S CHURCH-YARD.

1829.

TO

W. WHITMORE, Esq. M.P.

IN TOKEN OF ACKNOWLEDGMENT

OF HIS ABLE AND DISINTERESTED EFFORTS

IN FAVOUR OF

THE FREE TRADE OF INDIA,

AND IN THE HOPE OF FURTHER ANIMATING

AND EXPANDING HIS EXERTIONS

IN A CAUSE

WHICH IS NO LESS WORTHY OF THE STATESMAN,

THAN OF THE PHILANTHROPIST,

THESE PAGES ARE

RESPECTFULLY INSCRIBED.

# INTRODUCTION.

---

THE object of the following pages is not to enter upon the difficult, and almost unbounded, field of discussion, relatively to the affairs of India, but rather to attract public attention to the perilous situation of our empire in that quarter, with a view to the adoption of such measnres as may appear calculated to consolidate its strength, and to prepare it for the eventful crisis which, at no distant period, it must have to encounter. Several of the topics here touched upon, are so ably discussed in the work on "Colonial Policy as applicable to the Government of India," that the Author feels himself called upon to account for his having introduced them at all. He can only say, that as he considered them incidental to his subject, he did not think himself at liberty to avoid them altogether; and that, differing as he does only in a very slight degree from the writer alluded to, he shall feel himself amply rewarded if any of his readers, who happen not to have perused the above-named work, shall be induced to study it, in order to make themselves fully acquainted with the whole system of Indian Policy; for a work which has stronger claims to general attention, or which is better calculated to become the text-book of all who take a special interest in the affairs of India, is nowhere to be found.

On the subject of the Freedom of the Press, too, the Author has deemed it unnecessary, in the present concurrence of all the liberal and reflecting in the propriety and necessity of establishing such a principle, to add his feeble voice to the almost general acclaim. "No man who hath tasted learning," saith Milton, "but will confess the many ways of profiting by those who, not contented with stale receipts, are able to manage and set forth new positions to the world; and were they but as the dust and cinders of our feet, so long as in that notion they may yet serve to polish and brighten the armoury of truth, even for that respect they were not utterly to be cast away. But if they be of those whom God hath fitted for the special use of these times with eminent and ample gifts, and those perhaps neither among the priests nor among the Pharisees, and we, in the haste of a precipitant zeal, shall make no distinction, but resolve to stop their mouths, because we fear they come with new and dangerous opinions, as we commonly fore-judge them ere we understand them; no less than so to us, while, thinking thus to defend the Gospel, we are found the persecutors! This I know, that errors in a good government and in a bad are equally almost incident; for what magistrate may not be misinformed, and much the sooner, if liberty of printing be reduced into the power of a few? But to redress willingly and speedily what hath been erred, and in highest authority to esteem a plain advertisement more than others have done a sumptuous bribe, is a virtue (honoured Lords and Commons) answerable to your highest actions, and whereof none can participate but greatest and wisest men."* To the truth of such sentiments neither the lapse of time nor the ingenuity of man has been able to oppose any rational objections.

On the only remaining subject concerning India, the expiration of the Company's Charter, it would perhaps be premature to hazard any observations at the present moment. That momentous question must shortly be discussed; but as yet, facts, and not reasoning, are principally required. The periodical renewal of this question is considered by some as answering the effect which is aimed at by Machiavel, when, speaking of the instability of human institutions, he observes, that "those systems of government are best constituted, and continue longest, which either have establishments or institutions of their own, by the application of which they may be reduced to their first principles; or easily fall by accident, as it were, into some course that tends to such a renovation."†

* Areopagitica.

† Political Discourses, chap. i. book 3.

But Sydney, in reasoning upon this passage, very justly observes, that they who proposed doing this, "ought to have examined whether that principle be good or evil; or so good, that nothing can be added to it, which none ever was."* And certain it is, that in the instance of the Company's charter, what is termed the previous question, is of much more importance than a discussion of the conditions on which their lease should be renewed. Such a mass of vested rights, as well as of rights by prescription, have now grown up and blended themselves with the existence of the charter, that the voice of reason stands but an indifferent chance, when opposed to the clamours of interest, backed by the weight of political influence. Unhappily, too, those who are chiefly concerned, the natives of India, have no share in the debate, excepting by means of the few disinterested individuals who spontaneously advocate their cause; and of the latter, a very small portion is in the possession of wealth or influence: for as the wealth of an Indian has generally been accumu-

* Discourses on Government, p. 406.

lated by the operation of Indian abuses, it is but too frequently employed in continuing them.

How long, then, the present system is destined to continue—how long our fellow-subjects in India will have to defray the expenses of four distinct governments, or to pay an enormous surplus revenue, as a contribution towards the profit and loss of their chartered rulers, it is in vain to conjecture; but whatever be the determination on these points, that something may be done to ameliorate the condition of the inhabitants of our Eastern territories generally, is most earnestly to be desired, for the honour of human nature, as well as for the real interest of the British empire.

# CONTENTS.

# REFLECTIONS,

*&c.*

---

## CHAPTER I.

### ON THE TERRITORIAL ACQUISITIONS OF THE ENGLISH IN HINDOSTAN, AND THEIR POSITION AMONGST THE SOVEREIGN POWERS OF ASIA.

> "Memorare possem quibus in locis maxumas hostium copias populus Romanus parvâ manu fuderit; quas urbes, naturâ munitas, pugnando ceperit; ni ea res longius nos ab incœpto traheret."

THE history of the rise and progress of British influence in Hindostan has been so frequently written, that in offering any observation on the present situation of the East India Company, it is only necessary to advert to a few of the most prominent points of that eventful record. Most English writers on the affairs of India, contemplating with a very natural complacency the vast fabric which has been raised in so distant a part of the globe, by the enterprise and ability of their countrymen, have been led to overlook, if not to undervalue, the exploits of other European nations in the same field of exertion, and have easily persuaded themselves to believe that none but Englishmen could have acquired so extensive, and, apparently, so firmly-rooted a dominion. The general impression which they thus endeavour to convey, is not only inconsistent with that character for impartiality which history ought to uphold, but, at the present moment, is pregnant with the most mischievous effects, as tending to bias our speculations concerning the future government of so interesting a portion of the British Empire. It is easy to proceed from generals to particulars, and to satisfy those who are already sufficiently hostile to any change, that as Britain has shown itself the most able, because the most successful, candidate for supreme power in Hindostan, so her empire having been acquired under the ostensible agency of the India Company, that Company, under a renewal of their privileges, will be best able to preserve it. On this account, it would not be without its use, at the commencement of the ensuing discussions, to lay before the public a succinct but impartial statement of the exploits of the Portuguese, Dutch, and French, in the course of their several attempts to establish themselves in the continent of India. But as the investigation would involve nothing short of a general history of all the European settlements in that part of the world, it is sufficient, perhaps, on the present occasion, to refer to the pages of Di Barros and Raynal, as excellent correctives of our national historians; and to intimate that the exploits and noble conduct of Duarts Pacicco, with his small but intrepid band of heroes, in defence of Coction, against the King of Calicut; or of Francisco D'Almeida, and his gallant son Don Sorengo; or, above all, of the great Alphonso Albuquerque at Ormus, Goa, and Malacca, achievements which were even less honourable to his memory than the title of Just, which his great and eminent qualities extorted even from his enemies—will not readily meet a parallel, and certainly will not be surpassed, in the highest page of the Chronicle of the East India Company.

It is an error more frequently committed by those who merely record military events, than by the writers of general history, to allow their attention to be so entirely absorbed, by a desire to augment the fame of their favourite heroes, as to lead them to deny that the enemy had any qualities to entitle him to respect; forgetting that the merit of success rises in proportion to the obstacles opposed to it by his skill and courage. The contrary to this, however, appears to be the case with the narrators of the actions of Europeans in India, and a disposition is everywhere apparent to magnify the triumphs of a disciplined force over an ill-armed and tumultuous rabble, into matter of national renown and congratulation. This observation does not apply to the Portuguese, because their numbers were so exceedingly small, as to render even their escape from such overwhelming masses as they were opposed to, a subject of the greatest surprise and admiration; but, brilliant as their exploits undoubtedly were, and making every allowance for the national degeneracy which had then begun to display itself, they must cede the palm of intrepidity to the Dutch, who conquered the conquerors, and, under the command of Jacob Hemskerke, Gibrand Warwick, Stephen Vanhagen, and others, deprived them, after a short but severe struggle, of almost all the conquests and influence which they had acquired in India. But, if not to the Portuguese, it must be admitted that the observation applies to a great part of the military history of the English in Hindostan; and certainly, if they had not been opposed to the French, in the early part of their career, the renown of their conquest would have been less brilliant in proportion to the indifferent character for military prowess of the only enemy with whom they would then have had to contend.

The real cause of our success,* and the gene-

* Sir John Malcolm, in the introduction to his Political History of India, observes, that the means by which India was rendered subject to England, were, of all others, the best calculated to effect that great object. "Force and power," he says, "would not have approached the shores of India without meeting with resistance; but to the unpretending merchant every encouragement was afforded," &c. This observation, however, is peculiarly unfortunate, for no Europeans (even not excepting the Portuguese) ever approached India more by the operation of force and power than the English. Their first regular voyage, in 1601, after the Portuguese had been in possession of their extensive influence in India for more than a century, was signalised by the capture of one of that nation's largest vessels. Ten years after they forced an entrance into Surat, after worsting the Portuguese fleet, and obtained permission to erect factories. The fact is, that the length and danger of the voyage to India placed all adventurers under the necessity of embarking in the trade with ships both well armed and well manned; but the English, above all others, were attentive to fortify themselves on shore, and erect factories wherever they were able to establish themselves; and a very few years after their first settlement at Surat, we find them entering into a treaty with the Dutch to pay half the expenses of the garrison of Pullicat, besides maintaining ten ships of war in the Indian seas. The expenses of their factories and fortifications were, indeed, objected to as early as 1668, and contracts with the Native merchants recommended.—See Mill, vol. i p. 62, 3.

ral ascendency we have acquired in India, does not reside in our national character as Englishmen, but in the moral and physical energy which the arts of civilization confer on mankind, and in which it is the peculiar distinction of Europe to exhibit a marked contrast to the degenerate effeminacy of the greater part of the Asiatic continent. Long previous to the appearance of the English on the Peninsula of India, the inhabitants of that extensive region had felt, and acknowledged, the effect of European valour and discipline. Our countrymen had only to repeat the lesson which had but lately been impressed upon the minds of the Natives by the hardy achievements already alluded to. The question as to the

From the first the English had shown themselves more than a match for the Portuguese,—and from the Dutch they were fortunately relieved, in a great measure, by the superior importance which their formidable rivals attached to the spice trade of the Indian Archipelago; whilst the French, who appeared upon the stage when our countrymen had already become firmly settled, and, besides obtaining the cession of Bombay, had distinguished themselves against the Mahrattas —set the first example of aspiring to political influence, grounded upon cessions of territory from the Mogul Emperor. In short, the very reverse of Sir John Malcolm's observation appears to hold good, and the English may be said to owe their success to their *not* having approached India as unpretending merchants, but as warlike adventurers, aided by force and power.

competency of an Indian army to cope with even a vastly inferior force of disciplined Europeans, was already settled. After the first encounter this could never, indeed, have been for a moment doubtful; and, at the present day, it may be asserted, without fear of contradiction, that notwithstanding the long intercourse which the people of the Eastern world, whether under British influence or not, have had with the English, and with other Europeans—and notwithstanding the numerous opportunities which they have had of profiting by the examples placed before them, there is not a nation from Persia to China, that could oppose greater obstacles to the progress of an European army, than were experienced in the early period of our reign, when General Goddard marched across the Peninsula.

The struggle for supremacy, then, was not in reality a struggle between Europeans and Natives, but between European rivals amongst themselves; and from the instant the command of the ocean was obtained by the British, that struggle was at an end. Dupleix, Bussy, and Suffrein, did much to retard the event; but as the main contest between England and France was decided in Europe, those eminent men did but vainly strive against events which were totally beyond their control. Their efforts, indeed, rather tended to the advantage of the English Company, for it was the policy adopted by Dupleix, that first suggested that wide departure from the mercantile character, which eventually placed us in the position we now occupy amongst the powers of India. The appointment of that able man to the Soubahdarry of the Carnatic, by Salabut Jung, in 1755, and the cession which his equally distinguished colleague, Bussy, obtained from the same Prince, of a part of the Northern Circars, for the French Company, were the prelude and pretence for the English India Company's soliciting the title of Dewan of Bengal. Indeed, if the course of European politics had not taught the French commanders rather to indulge their feelings of national rivalry, than to attend to the prudent line of conduct which their relative position in India ought to have suggested, they would probably have avoided coming into direct collision with their powerful competitors; in which case, they would have preserved an influence in India, which even our great maritime resources might not have enabled us easily to destroy. Under this supposition, what the result might have been if the French had retained Surat, and directed all their efforts to advance in the line of the Nerbudda, or even the Indus, would be a curious, though now a fruitless speculation.

But, whatever might have been the event, if the decisive struggle had been deferred until the rival Companies had been more nearly on an equality as to their available resources, no man can doubt that the conqueror was destined to be Lord of the Indian World. By the discovery of a passage round the Cape of Good Hope, the weakest, and most effeminate portion of the globe, was, in a manner, laid open to the attacks of the strongest and most enterprising. The exploits of the Greek mercenaries, the Macedonian conquest, and even the comparatively feeble inroads of the Romans in the decline of the Empire, had never failed to evince the effect of military discipline, when fairly brought to bear on the countless array of an Asiatic force; and if this is undeniable as an historical fact, relatively to that portion of the Eastern World, which, being in immediate contact with the Western, was likely to have imbibed some share of its warlike character and principles of organization, how much more certain is it, that the same effect could not but follow in a quarter, the remoteness of which from any such source of improvement conspired, with an enervating climate, to render its inhabitants both morally and physically an easy prey to the first invader. Accordingly, we find that the conflict between civilization and semi-barbarism; between the degeneracy attendant upon vicious institutions, and the spirit of enterprise resulting from freedom and intellectual energy, was never for an instant doubtful. The same tide of success by which the progress of the Spaniards was characterised in America, carried forward the British in their conquest of Hindostan; and if, in either case, that tide seemed for a moment to be interrupted, it was only when the confidence or arrogance of the victor induced him to rely too much on his courage or good fortune; in short, to despise every indication of a warlike spirit on the part of his opponents.

With such a prey, then, within their grasp—so rich in attraction—so powerless to defend itself—it is evident that there was no conceivable limit to the career of our countrymen, but in the restraints which the great council of the nation might see fit to impose upon them. The want of the necessary funds, which, at first sight, promised to become a barrier to their advance, became, in fact, the principal inducement to their aggressions, and, occasionally, furnished them with the means of extending them. So many petty usurpations had started up, when the Mogul Empire was dismembered, that the British, who made their appearance at that crisis of intrigue and rivalry, not only found every facility in compassing their own more legitimate ends, but were tempted by many an Indian Divitiacus to push forward their invincible legions, and to interfere in the politics of the country, by those splendid offers of remuneration which the traitors were enabled to hold out, by intercepting the provincial treasures on their passage to the capital. It cannot be denied that it required an arduous exertion of self-denial to decline opportunities at once so tempting in point of immediate profit, and attended, in reality, with so little risk: in this sense it is no doubt true, that the first advance of the English, from their several factories, was decisive of their future conduct, and the position in which they found themselves was, certainly, little calculated to encourage the adoption of any system of policy, founded upon a just and equitable estimate of the claims of the various powers with whom they were thus suddenly brought in contact.

If the hope of gain, however, tempted the agents of the Company to embroil themselves with the Native Powers, their profusion and imprudence did not fail to involve them, shortly after, in the greatest financial difficulties. An inordinate thirst for commercial profit characterised them as merchants, and an eager desire to silence the scruples and reproaches of the home authorities, by exhibiting a show of revenue as an excuse for their political enterprises, was the line of policy subsequently pursued. At first they merely stipulated with their Indian allies for an exemption from duty on their merchandize; but afterwards, when they began to mix more intimately in the intrigues of the petty chiefs around them, they became willing accomplices whenever the prospect of adequate advantage was held forth; and *point d'argent point de Suisse*, would then have been a much more appropriate motto than the imposing one since adopted, without, it is to be hoped, the sanction of the British Senate. It had been well, indeed, if the possession of wealth had been their only ambition; but when the immense hoards of treasure, accumulated and plundered throughout the Empire, were entirely exhausted in the payment of their heavy demands, the animosity and ambition of the Native Chiefs still remaining unappeased, a convenient substitute was found in land, and a district, yielding a certain revenue, became, in most cases, the stipulation agreed upon. But as it is a much easier task to cede territory than to give quiet possession of it,—to estimate the amount of revenue, than to point out how that revenue is to be collected, the territorial acquisitions of the Company almost invariably brought with them the necessity for expelling some occupant, whose title was, not unfrequently, more valid than that of the power assuming to be paramount, and of burthening the unhappy population with taxes, in addition to those which had already reduced them to the greatest poverty.

Nor were these the only embarrassments in which the foreign transactions of the Company involved them. The several Presidencies of Bengal, Madras, and Bombay, acting upon views of local expediency, or of apparent commercial advantage, were sometimes in direct opposition to each other, and always exhibited, to the nations of Hindostan, the spectacle of a people actuated by every impulse of pecuniary or political covetousness. Thus at Bombay, a league with the Mahrattas, the enemies of the Mogul, for the protection of our trade against Angria the pirate,—and with the Mogul authorities themselves against the Mahrattas,—signalized the commencement of our career in that part of India; and the violation of the treaty of Poorundur, and the disavowal of the convention of Wargaum, soon followed. Thus the Company offered its assistance alternately to those who rebelled against their lawful sovereign, and to that sovereign himself, just as its interest at the moment happened to prompt:—witness the deposition of Surajah-ul-Dowlah and of Meer Jaffier,—the alliance with the Mogul against Cossim Alli,—the deposition of the latter, and the restoration of Meer Jaffier, after the latter had been stigmatized by them as an avaricious ruler, whose chief officers sought only to enrich themselves by the plunder of the people, who had occasioned a scarcity and dearness of provisions in his country by the heavy and exorbitant taxes which he had levied, and whose conduct, in short, made him the dread and detestation of all good men, and called aloud for a change of system:—witness their subsequent opposition to the Mogul himself, till bought off by a promise of the cession of Oude, then ruled by Surajah-ul-Dowlah, who himself, however, shortly after purchased their alliance for fifty lacs of rupees, and availed himself of their aid to crush the Rohillas, without the shadow of a reason beyond the 'fixed hate and loathing' which he bore the posterity of Ali Mohammed, the principal founder of their clan, and the personal enemy of his father:—witness, also, their disgusting arrogance and injustice towards Mahomed Ali, Nabob of the Carnatic, who had evinced his gratitude for their support, in fixing him in his dignity, by contributing the treasures left him by his father, his own large resources, and all that he could raise upon credit, as a fund to meet the expenses of the war with the French, as well as for the re-establishment of their ruined factories in Bengal,—conduct which left an indelible stain, not only on the reputation of the Company, but on that of the British nation, by whom the rights of the Nabob had been unequivocally and solemnly acknowledged in the treaty of Paris in 1763. Thus, too, on the Coromandel coast, national rivalry was the occasion and excuse for the agents of the Company endeavouring to ruin the French interest at the Native Courts, by their intrigues; and the cession of the Northern Circars, in 1765, was the fruit of this policy; whilst at Calcutta, a thirst for dominion and pecuniary profit obtained Bengal, Behar, and Orissa, about the same time, under a promise of the payment of twenty-six lacs of rupees annually to the Mogul, which tribute, though exceedingly small when compared with the revenues of those provinces, was withheld, in less than eight years, under the pretext that the unfortunate Monarch, who it was notorious was not master of his own actions, had broken his agreement with the Company, by consenting to reside in the capital of his Empire, under the protection of the Mahrattas. And to conclude, when Sir John Lindsay, and afterwards Sir Robert Harland, were sent out from Europe as commissioners and plenipotentiaries, to ensure the execution of the treaty of Paris, to which our ally, Mahomed Ali, as well as Salabut Jung, Soubahdar of the Deccan, were in some measure considered as parties, their presence was found so inconvenient by the Council of Madras, that every possible obstruction was thrown in their way, and their recall earnestly, and, to the disgrace of the nation, successfully recommended. The selection of those individuals does not indeed appear to have been a happy one; but much allowance should be made for them, in consequence of the various and even impracticable engagements with the Native Powers, with which the Company's Government had embarrassed itself:—they determined to cut the knot which it was so difficult to untie; but in so doing, they ran the risk of committing even a greater injustice than that which they desired to correct. Placed in a novel situation, with extensive but imperfectly defined powers, the Commissioners were probably inclined, like the Supreme Court of Judicature on its first establishment in Bengal, to interfere too much in the ordinary administration of the Provinces; but their presence, under more precise regulations, if they had been men of greater ability and experience, would still have been eminently useful, as a check upon those proceedings of the Company's Government, which so frequently entailed the deepest disgrace upon the national character.* The experiment might still be made with every prospect of advantage.

But whatever may have been the injury done to our national character, it cannot be denied that it is to a steady adherence to the system of political barter just described, that the Company owes its extensive territories. Nothing was done without an equivalent, either in money, or in land, rated at an annual revenue greatly exceeding the interest of the outlay attending its acquisition; and it is susceptible of proof, that if commercial had not been blended with political transactions,

* Hyder Ali is said to have declared that peace with the English was indifferent to him, since they had shown themselves totally unworthy of confidence. The splendid passage in Burke's Speech on the Nabob of Arcot's Debts, 28th Feb. 1785, is well known:—"When at length Hyder Ali found that he had to do with men who either would sign no convention, or whom no treaty and no signature could bind, and who were the determined enemies of human intercourse itself, he decreed to make the country, possessed by these incorrigible and predestinated criminals, a memorable example to mankind. He resolved, in the gloomy recesses of a mind capacious of such things, to leave the whole Carnatic an everlasting monument of vengeance, and to put perpetual desolation as a barrier between him and those against whom the faith which holds the moral elements of the world together was no protection."

the British power in India would now exhibit the singular spectacle, of a government continually at war, and yet totally free from public debt. The statements published by Mr. Rickards have clearly shown, that whilst the utmost prosperity attended the Company, even in its most unjustifiable aggressions upon the neighbouring States, its trade was so improvidently conducted as to threaten absolute bankruptcy—a crisis which seems only to have been averted by the appropriation of territorial revenue to the amount of a million sterling per annum, or, in other words, the imposition of a tax to that amount upon their Indian subjects. The whole of the dividends paid to proprietors of India stock for a period of seventeen years, prior to the last renewal of the Company's charter, may, indeed, be said to have been furnished by money extorted from the people of Hindostan, by a system of the most oppressive taxation probably ever inflicted upon any country in the world—a taxation so heavy, and so directly tending to the impoverishment of the wretched inhabitants, as to cause a doubt in the minds of reflecting men whether we are not called upon, in justice and in mercy, to relinquish altogether the possession of a country, the Government of which is so much more expensive than its actual resources are able to support.

But independent of political consideration, the difficulties attending the abandonment of territory, particularly after it has been for any considerable period under our sway, are more than sufficient to outweigh the humane motives upon which such a measure might be suggested. To whom, in fact, are we to restore such conquests? If the authorities from whom we wrested them, we should merely relieve the inhabitants from one set of usurpers, to deliver them into the hands of a worse; with the aggravation, too, of the latter being both exasperated and impoverished in consequence of those changes which they believe the English to have been principally instrumental in bringing about. There is not, perhaps, a square mile of territory, from Cape Comorin to the Himalayah mountains, that had not for very considerable periods been subject, under some form or other, directly or indirectly, to foreign dynasties or usurpers; and it was but in comparatively few instances, that the dismemberment of the Mogul empire gave the actual possessors a more valid claim, than that acquired by the Company in the course of their negotiations or conquests. The reproach of the Company is not in its having appropriated as large a share of the spoil as it could secure, by treaty, or by force of arms, after it had declared itself a political competitor; but in having associated itself with miscreants and traitors, and, by alternately employing meanness and arrogance, open force, and treacherous intrigue, having effected its guilty purpose. To talk, then, of restoring possessions acquired under such circumstances, is to inculcate at least a very questionable morality, and to advocate the opinion, that provided our conscience be quieted by such a measure, the subsequent fate of the helpless natives need not give us the slightest uneasiness. We have seen, however, too many instances of the consequence of such a step; and a scene is now acting on the banks of the Irrawaddy, which should for ever banish all thoughts of adopting a line of conduct, which, under the guise of magnanimity, is in reality an act of the basest and most cruel desertion. It is well known, that the inhabitants of Pegue were encouraged to afford their assistance to the British army, by the proclamation published by Sir A. Campbell, in which he exhorts them, by every promise that could be supposed to tempt that nation, to revolt against such an iron sway as that of the Burmese. "Compare," says the British Commander, "your condition with the comfort and happiness of the poor maritime provinces, viz. Mergui, Yeah, Tavoy, and Martaban, now under the protection of the English flag; follow their example to enjoy their blessings, by placing yourselves under my protection; it is a duty you owe to your aged and infirm parents, to your female relatives, your wives and children."—On being assured that this proclamation really emanated from authority, for they deputed one of their chiefs expressly to make the inquiry, the major part of them came over to the British Army, many of them bringing their arms with them; and during the remainder of the war co-operated with our forces. Yet, after having thus, upon the faith of our promises, incurred the deepest resentment of their unforgiving foes, the Burmese, they were again delivered over to the tender mercies of the Lord of the White Elephant, with merely the hollow provision in their favour, contained in the sixth article of the treaty of peace, that "no person whatever, whether native or foreigner, is hereafter to be molested by either party, on account of the part which he may have taken, or have been compelled to take, in the present war." The sequel is known to every body who has found leisure to devote a few moments' attention to what passes in so remote a part of the globe. Those who escaped the sword fell by the hands of the executioner, unless they averted their fate by the payment of such heavy fines as reduced them to a mass of abject and powerless slaves—

themselves and all they hold dear kept, as the fatal proclamation described them, "in constant terror of their lives, and, like wild beasts, frequenting jungles." And such, doubtless, would be the lot of the inhabitants of India, generally, whenever any considerable portion of the territory should be abandoned by the British authorities.* The Mahometan, assisted by crowds of Arab mercenaries —the Seik—the Nepaulese—the Mahratta, and even the Burmese, would carve, each for himself, an empire over the less energetic inhabitants of the peninsula. The greater, as well as most fruitful portion of India, bounded as it is by nations which are robust and warlike, in comparison with the inhabitants of the plains, is unfit for

* The abandonment of the Rajhpoot states in 1805, in consequence of the line of policy imposed upon Lord Cornwallis, and his successor Sir George Barlow, it is well known, consigned that unfortunate race to the avarice and extortion of the Mahrattas, and their ally Amir Khan; and it is worthy of remark, that when those states were again taken under the protection of the British Government, it was only on condition of the greater part of them paying to the Company the same tributes, in fact, that had been exacted by the Mahrattas. This, indeed, was stated to be in return for political protection, and military defence, but the whole of the Mahratta powers having been completely prostrated by the masterly operations of Lord Hastings in 1818, that protection and defence were no longer necessary to their security.

the establishment of a government composed entirely of natives:—like the horse in the fable, they are incapable of putting forth their best speed, in the race of civilization, without the assistance of a rider to animate their exertions, and direct their course. When successfully defended, it has always been by foreigners—witness the numerous Patan dynasties by whom Bengal and Behar were so long maintained in independence, and who not only repulsed all attempts to subdue them, but even carried their arms beyond the Indus, and conquered Cabul and Candahar.

The natives of the plains, indeed, appear to be so insensible to that regard for the dignity of human nature, by which combinations for self-defence, and public institutions of all kinds, are encouraged,—they are as a body so deficient in that feeling of mutual confidence, upon which the power of self-government must depend, that it is quite impossible to believe them capable of defending themselves against the encroachments of their neighbours, in the event of the administration of the country being committed to their control. If such a step were taken, they would very shortly invoke the assistance of their late masters, and the groans of the Hindoos would place us under the necessity either of entangling ourselves once again in the politics of the country, or of witnessing the oppression of our former subjects, under the consciousness that our own government had done its utmost to incapacitate them from making any resistance.

On these principles, the resignation of any part of the Indian territory would be inconsistent with justice or even with sound policy, for in the event of a portion only being given up, its quick subjugation, by the most powerful of its neighbours, would only protract for a little the period when we should have to struggle for our own safety, and enter once more upon the arena of political contention. The expediency of such a step, though at all times furnishing an alluring topic of declamation, is applicable, if at all, only to such recent acquisitions, as, having been wrested from organised governments, and not always upon principles of self-defence, or under an expressed or implied obligation to protect them against former usurpers, do not involve either a national breach of faith, or such a sudden change in the settled state of society, as would occasion inconvenience, if not ruin, to the majority of the community.

The fact indeed seems to be, that in a country so unsettled as India was at the time of the English appearing in it,—in a country, too, so remarkably deficient in that public spirit and character to be acquired by civilization alone, it was very difficult for the East India Company to maintain a stationary position. A certain degree of influence, and a small extent of independent territory, were absolutely necessary for its safety; and had these been secured upon a moderate scale, it might always have commanded advantages sufficient to preclude any apprehension of its being overawed by a native force; and the benefits of commerce being reciprocal, the surplus produce of the country would not have failed, in that case, to find its way into the English factories. To have constantly declined advancing, however, when allurements to ambition were everywhere held out, was more than could have been expected from a government administered by so many individuals of various talents and character, and by men whose distance from the Mother Country almost entirely relieved them from responsibility. When fairly committed in the great struggle for independence and power, no matter whether by the incapacity or the rashness of colleagues, the difficulty of preserving a strict neutrality, without a compromise of the national dignity, (a quality, alas! at once so palpable and so evanescent as to invite and yet to elude the attempts of every "brief authority" to define it) was enhanced, in proportion to the numbers of all ranks of natives who voluntarily resided under their protection. For it must not be concealed, that although the subjects of the Company have great reason to complain of the avaricious and oppressive nature of its government, yet it is still, in most of its features, very superior to any other which they could hope to enjoy by a change of masters. If it were otherwise, it would indeed be disgraceful to human nature; but, nevertheless, it should not be forgotten, that our duty is not restricted to giving the country a better government than it could expect under native rulers—we should give it the best, which, under all circumstances, it is capable of enjoying.

In despite, then, of the feeling of indignation which every honest mind must experience, on perusing a detail of the unworthy, and often criminal, means by which the East India Company have attained possession of their vast domains, it is impossible, without doing a still greater wrong, to counsel any other atonement * for the wrong already committed, than that which a just and liberal system of government will afford. If we can give peace, happiness, and security to

* The expediency of relinquishing our conquests in India, will, to most people, appear in the highest degree extravagant, even if it were possible to draw a line between what could be called the old, and the new acquisitions of the

those realms,—if we can rescue them from the state of degradation into which they have been plunged, no less by natural than by moral causes—by their effeminacy, as well as by their vices,—and if we can raise them to the rank of a free and an industrious people, then, and then only, will our dominion have been a blessing; in every other point of view it must be looked upon only as the means of perpetuating the misery of a wretched population of nearly a hundred millions, and of entailing a heavy and indelible disgrace upon the British name.

Company. In the wide field of Indian speculation, however, there are not wanting those who do counsel such a measure.—*In eodem prato, bos herbam quærit, canis leporem, ciconia lacertum.*—A few words therefore, on the point in question, it was thought, would not be deemed irrelevant.

## CHAPTER II.

### ON THE DANGER TO WHICH BRITISH INDIA IS EXPOSED FROM INVASION.

"La vostra nominanza è color d'erba
Che viene, e va, e quei la discolora
Per cui ell' esce della terra acerba."

THE view just taken of the nature of our Indian empire, suggests these two important inquiries.—What are the dangers to which Hindostan is exposed in the event of its being invaded by a powerful enemy capable of meeting a British army in the field? and, What degree of attachment can the Natives be supposed to bear to our name and government? Upon the first of these points, a few observations will form the subject of the present chapter.

The most careless reader of Indian history cannot have failed to observe, that every Asiatic people, with whom the British forces have come into contact, have shown themselves unable to resist the European system of war and discipline.

Yet past exploits, and the transactions under the administrations of Lords Wellesley and Minto, were not of themselves sufficiently decisive upon this head, to convince those who had taken a superficial view of the causes of our success; and the then impending conflict with Nepaul, which may be said to have been bequeathed as a state legacy to Lord Hastings, was by many considered to be the *experimentum crucis* of the military character of the Indian government. So, indeed, it proved to be, as far as tactics and discipline were concerned; for it was by our superiority on those points alone that the struggle was decided in our favour. The Nepaulese were superior in physical strength, if not in personal courage, to the greater part of our troops; they had numbers at their command, and their country abounded in natural obstacles and defensive positions; yet by the effect of comprehensive military arrangement, assisted by good discipline, were all these advantages set at nought, and the war, so formidable in its first aspect, brought to a successful termination in two short campaigns. Still, although the splendid government of Lord Hastings achieved this great and important triumph, which, in addition to those masterly operations which his Lordship directed against the Mahrattas and Pindarries, appeared to place the Company's territories in a state of permanent security, there yet remained one enemy with whom the Indian army had not measured its strength; and as Lord Minto had left the war of Nepaul to him, so Lord Hastings left that of Ava to his successor. In the event, however, the Burmese proved to be even less formidable than any antagonist whom the British had hitherto been tempted to meet in the field; and the dismemberment of their empire, together with the establishment of military stations in Cachar, Arracan, and on the borders of Pegue, effectually put it out of their power to molest the Bengal government in future, even if their contemptible character, in a military point of view, did not render the occurrence of such a contingency comparatively unimportant. Thus, while the interior of India is entirely under British influence or authority, the whole frontier of that vast tract is tenanted by states, which not only have felt the weight of our arms, but which have been compelled to admit resident officers at their courts, or in their immediate vicinity, to watch over and report upon their conduct. The Seiks, who witnessed the operations of the British army in 1805, and have since acknowledged our influence, form no material exception to this general arrangement.

Whether it be in consequence of the influence of climate, or of imperfect social institutions, or, as is more probable, of both, it is observable that the Asiatic nations have shown themselves less susceptible of consistent and sustained exertions of warlike skill, in proportion as the country which they inhabit approaches towards the tropics. The sun, which imparts its fire and vivacity to them, seems to deny them the exercise of judgment and discretion. Even the natural advantages of a strong country appear to form no exception to the truth of this remark; and whilst the mountaineers of Nepaul excel the inhabitants of the hilly regions of Southern India, including Ceylon, the latter made a much firmer stand against the Moguls and the English, than the tribes established in the fastnesses of Java have shown themselves capable of in their resistance to the Dutch.* Many of the nations now alluded to had acquired considerable knowledge in the arts of war and government; the Nepaulese and Burmese had subjugated several neighbouring states and provinces; but the latter, in particular,

* By recent advices, however, it would appear that the extremely weak state of the European establishments of the Dutch in Java, has at length tempted the natives of that island to rise and make strenuous efforts to recover their independence. If the character here given of the Southern Asiatics does not operate to the disadvantage of the Javanese, we may shortly hear of the Dutch being totally expelled the island.

after pursuing the career of conquest with remarkable spirit for a series of years, had apparently become contented with what they had acquired, and, without evincing any genius for improvement, had deteriorated in the stupid tyranny of their domestic government, in proportion as they had relaxed from the energy of their foreign policy. It seems, indeed, to be a law of nature, that nothing in the history of mankind shall be stationary: to cease to advance in the career of improvement, is to retrograde; and thus we invariably find, that the half-civilized portions of the globe, when no longer acted upon by their first impulse, become alike the prey either of the civilized portion, on the one hand, or of the complete barbarian on the other. Thus the half-civilized states of China, Persia, and Hindostan, showed themselves as unable to resist the barbarian Tartar tribes, as the Asiatics of modern times have been to withstand the attacks of European invaders; whilst the Tartar conquerors, in their turn, when they came to partake of the half-civilized character of the conquered, evinced themselves utterly incompetent to withstand the discipline and organized institutions of Great Britain and Russia.

The same reasoning, which is applicable to the English in their present attitude as an Asiatic power, is equally so to Russia; with this consideration, indeed, which gives additional force to it, that the latter is in a manner compelled, by her natural position, to that collision with the weaker states, which the former has traversed half the globe to provoke. It is evident, however, that the same train of consequences must in both cases attend upon the conflict between a people rapidly advancing in civilization, and one, if not in the act of retrograding, certainly almost stationary; and that, in proportion as the southern provinces of the Russian empire profit by the attention which is bestowed upon them by the government, the Autocrat of the North will be assailed by the same temptations to aggrandize himself at the expense of his semi-barbarous neighbours, which the East India Company's agents were unable to resist in their progress towards the conquest of Hindostan. Nor are the facilities which the Russians enjoy for the prosecution of such enterprises, at all inferior to those which their superior maritime strength conferred upon the English. The water-communication between the Baltic and the Caspian is complete and uninterrupted: from St. Petersburgh to the Neva, a canal runs along the margin of Lake Ladoga to the Walkowa, from which the navigation is continued by the Nesta and the Sna, to another canal which joins the Tuertsa, of which the waters flow into the Wolga; so that military stores can be conveyed, with comparatively small risk or expense, not only to the southern and eastern shores of the Caspian, but probably to the centre of Khorasan, or to the confines of Cabul.

In weighing the inducements which are thus held out to Russia to aggrandize herself, it cannot but be perceived that the great prize at which she aims must undoubtedly be Hindostan. Persia, and the countries immediately contiguous, offer comparatively but a feeble temptation; the barren soil of the former, and its deficiency in navigable streams, render it unfit for colonization, and worthless as a conquest; whilst the tracts lying between Orenberg and Balkh contain so great a proportion of desert and uninhabitable land, that, notwithstanding the advantages to be derived from the fine streams which flow into the Sea of Aral and the Caspian, any extensive settlement in that quarter would be a work of time and difficulty. It is probable, then, that Russia would covet no more of either than to afford her a safe and easy communication with the territories immediately adjacent to India. The whole line of her frontier, from the Seas of Kamtschatka and

Okhotsk to the Caspian, is so well guarded by the cautious policy of the Chinese, no less than by natural obstacles, that, taking into consideration the scanty population and bleak climate of Siberia, together with the difficulty of assembling a large force in those quarters, there can be little encouragement for her to attempt an advance in that direction. But when her frequent wars with Turkey and Persia are considered; the armies so long concentrated in Georgia and Armenia; the military colonies planted in her southern provinces, together with the now long-established habits of the people of those parts, which have reconciled them to the inconvenience of their situation, and taught them to meet the exigencies attendant upon so warlike a neighbourhood, we cannot but perceive that, whether from the elasticity of an increasing population,* or from the wish to employ large masses of troops, which it might be alike expensive and dangerous to remand to the northern provinces, the country

* See the Chevalier Gamba's Account of Georgia, for the encouragement afforded to commerce and agriculture by the Russian Government, and the immense accession to the population from the neighbouring provinces of the Persian and Turkish empires. In 1820, seven thousand families are said to have gone over to the Russian dominions.

extending towards our Eastern possessions is the line of least resistance, and the direction in which the explosion must take place.

On the other hand, if to the operation of natural causes, as just described, we add the stimulus of political rivalry, we may be assured that every circumstance conspires to produce the collision of Great Britain and Russia on the confines of India, and that at no very distant period. Russia, at least, will leave nothing unattempted to accelerate the meeting, or rather to place the occurrence of that meeting entirely at her own option in point of time; for in what other quarter can she detect a vulnerable point in the armour of her mighty antagonist, or where could she desire a nobler field on which to measure her colossal strength with her undaunted rival, than on the plain of Hindostan?

In discussing the probability of such an attack being made upon India, the mind naturally recurs to the Macedonian conquest; and with reference to the loosely-recorded enterprise of Alexander, we form, perhaps, an exaggerated estimate of the length of the march, the difficulties of the road, and the hostile dispositions of the nations whose territory would have to be traversed. Making allowances for the improvement of modern warfare, this might, indeed, be the correct mode of reasoning, in the event of such an expedition as that which is said to have been meditated by Napoleon, after the conquest of Egypt; but great is the difference between the obstacles to be overcome on such a route, and those which oppose themselves to a march from the shores of the Caspian. On consulting the map, we may observe that the Russian possessions already extend very nearly to the spot whence most of the later conquerors of Hindostan set out on their route. The geography of that part of Asia is still so imperfectly known, that it has not yet been clearly ascertained whether the river upon which stands the city of Herat, disembogues itself into the Caspian by the Gulf of Balkan, or joins the Oxus in its course to the Sea of Aral. If, however, as is most probable, the former be the fact, an establishment on the island of Naphtonia, or in the Gulf of Balkan, would place the Russians in communication with the Turcoman tribes, whose hostility to the Persians is deadly and hereditary, and secure the means of advancing by Herat to Cabul, without the necessity of taking the more circuitous route by the southern shores of the Caspian, or of following the more difficult track, already laid down, from Orenberg to the banks of the Oxus, and along the course of the Amu to Balkh. The Turcomans and Usbecs, though formidable to a nation so weak in itself, and so defective in military organization as the Persians, would be unable to oppose a large well-appointed army of Russians, even if their hopes of plunder did not induce them eagerly to take part in the expedition. If, however, it be thought that an advance through Azerbijan, and the north of Persia, into Khorasan, though the most tedious, would yet be the safest route, the progress which the Russian arms are now making in that direction,* afford every prospect of the way being very soon left open to them. Every conflict into which it is so easy for a powerful state to force its weaker neighbour, especially in a quarter so remote from general observation, and therefore so little liable to excite public animadversion, must of necessity end in defeat to the Persians, and, in consequence of their poverty, with reference to the probable demands of Russia, as well as to their misgovernment, in a cession of territory. Already has the feeble barrier of the Kur, and the Uras, been forced; and, in addition to their conquests, indemnification for the expenses of the war, may possibly place the Russians in possession of Ghilan

* If we may believe the latest intelligence, the Russians have taken possession of Tabriz, and are in full march upon Teheran, a point at least four hundred and fifty miles within the boundary, and on the route to Herat.

and Mazenderan, provinces which Peter the Great considered necessary to the establishment of his complete ascendency on the Caspian.

But it is not to war and conquest alone that we must look for the narrowing of that space which separates the two most powerful candidates, not only for the supremacy of Asia, but, through her, for preponderance in Europe also. For it is not to be doubted, that the possession of India would greatly increase the influence of Russia in the general councils of Europe—even its danger would probably have an unfavourable effect upon the politics of Great Britain. Nations, like individuals, to be honest must be independent: and, under the bare possibility of our Asiatic territories being wrested from us, it is not difficult to conjecture the unworthy compliances into which we may be driven. But by open war, however efficient in the end, this crisis might not, possibly, be produced for many years; notwithstanding the direct interest which Russia must have in silently acquiring that position, from which, eventually, she may be able to turn her attention towards India, without that previous "note of preparation," and hostility with neighbouring states, which her present situation would render unavoidable. A reference to the line of policy adopted by the East India Company, and the various means by which the whole country, from Cape Comorin to the Himalayah Mountains, has been reduced under the direct sway or acknowledged influence of the English, would readily suggest those measures by which a paramount control in Central Asia might be obtained with very little outward appearance of injustice or violence. The disputes which always attend the succession to the throne in Persia,* are fruitful in crimes, of which political hypocrisy might take advantage, to read a great moral lesson to that unfortunate nation; and such is the uncertainty of life, as well as right, among the members of the royal family, that any of them, whatever might be his pretensions, would gladly cede one half of the kingdom to an auxiliary who was powerful enough to secure him in the undisturbed possession of the remainder. This is by far the most rapid, as well as the most effectual mode, by which Russia can obtain that vantage ground which will enable her to affront the Eastern world. In order to accomplish a measure to her so desirable, the tranquillity of Europe, though of course favourable, is by no means indispensable; since the usual garrisons and provincial detachments, stationed in the

* By late accounts, it appears that the Shekakee tribe, the most powerful in Azerbijan, has joined the Russians: the father of Jehangir Khan, their chief, it will be recollected, disputed the crown with the present Shah.

neighbourhood of the Persian frontier, are at any time sufficient for the intimidation of a state, at once so uninformed in matters of political science, and so little entitled to respect on account of its military capabilities. By means of one of those treaties, which a power so formidable can always negotiate with one of the competitors for the throne of a nation torn by internal dissensions, and in momentary dread of the incursions of the fierce and lawless tribes in its vicinity, Russia might obtain by cession, or under the condition of a temporary occupation, or by means of a permanent subsidiary force, not only the command of as much territory as would be necessary to facilitate her advance upon the Indian frontier, but a stipulation for such farther aid in cattle, provisions, or men, as Persia might be able to afford. Such, indeed, is the unsettled state of the Shah's dominions, even in the most quiet times, that it may well be doubted if such a treaty, coupled as it would be with actual assistance and great moral influence in repressing insurrections of all kinds, would be mainly disadvantageous to him at any given period; but at the present moment, when the course of affairs in the western world tends, if not to the total expulsion of the Mohammedans from Europe, at least to a very great retrenchment of their power in that quarter, Persia may shortly feel the necessity of strengthening her western frontier, to guard against that re-action which the spirit of the Turkish Government will probably display when confined almost entirely to her Asiatic possessions. If Russia, therefore, were to exact the assistance of the reigning Shah, in subduing the country lying in the direct route to India by the Oxus and the Amu; or in acquiring military possession of Candahar, as the price of her support on the Tigris and Euphrates, and the confines of Kurdistan and Armenia; there would be little doubt of her success in the object she cannot but have most at heart,—that of bringing within the reach of her grasp the brightest jewel in the crown of her illustrious rival.

The route leading from Russia to the Indies is not, as before remarked, by the south of the Caspian and Khorasan alone, but may be traced out east of the Caspian, by Khiva and the course of the Oxus and Amu to Bokhara, Samarcand, and Balkh; or east of the Sea of Aral, by the Kirgies Desert, and the Sur, or Sihoon, to nearly the same point in the great line of trade established between eastern Russia and Central Asia. Indeed, there can be little doubt that the attention of the Court of Petersburgh has already been directed to this line, and that, whatever may have been the ostensible object of the recent Missions to Khiva and Bokhara, no ordinary anxiety has been evinced to ascertain how far an improvement in commercial intercourse might be turned to account in paving the way for the establishment of a political influence amongst hordes of barbarians, who, though apparently accessible to no kindness or conciliation, appear only to need the presence of some really formidable authority, to be reduced to the same state of tranquillity as the fierce and lawless inhabitants on the confines of Georgia and Armenia, and other districts into which Russia has successively introduced her system of rule.

But under whatever circumstances the invasion of India might be attempted, it is probable that the attacking army, instead of marching directly from Russia, would be composed principally of troops stationed in recent conquests, or in the employ of Persia, as a subsidiary force, or as an army of occupation. Thus the Russian troops, though apparently more closely connected with the parent country, are likely to lose much of their energy by a long sojourn in distant and, perhaps, uncongenial climes; and when to this circumstance is added the probability of a considerable admixture of Asiatic recruits, to fill up occasional vacancies, it may be supposed that the invading army would assimilate pretty nearly, as to its component parts, to the force which the English might be able to collect in defence of their possessions. Yet, supposing this to be the case, without any qualification, supposing the two armies to contain the same number of Europeans, the remainder being composed of natives of the countries in the possession of each nation respectively, still the advantage would rest with the invaders. A mixture of different nations in one army, if not permitted to impair its discipline, is no detriment to it, but probably the contrary, in offensive operations; but in defence, some feeling to counterbalance the effect of occasional failure is indispensable,—that feeling is patriotism: and it may be assumed as an axiom, that whilst, for invasion, an army may be composed of soldiers of one or of many nations, indifferently; for defence, every man in it ought to have a strong interest in the soil which he endeavours to protect.

In order, effectually, to oppose the invasion of India, it would be desirable to occupy the Punjab. That region once passed, there would no longer be any natural obstacles, of which the defenders could avail themselves, in opposing a direct advance into the heart of Hindostan. The Punjab, indeed, has always been the field in which the rulers of Delhi have defended themselves with the greatest advantage; when that is in possession of the enemy, no alternative remains to the invaded, beyond that of committing the fortune of the war to the event of one great battle on the plains of Kurnaul or Panniput—already too often fatal to Hindostan—or of allowing the enemy to ravage and lay waste the country, and to advance unmolested to the siege of Delhi, in the confidence that, even if unsuccessful, they will always have a strong country in their rear to retreat to and to encamp in, until the recurrence of the fair season for their operations, or the arrival of reinforcements from the other side of the Indus. On the other hand, the Indian army, by having the Punjab organized in its rear, would not only command the services of the warlike race inhabiting those tracts, but it would possess the advantage of receiving supplies by the Indus, and its tributary streams, instead of the circuitous route of the Bay of Bengal and the Ganges. The right flank of their army, too, would be greatly strengthened by the force which occupies the protected hill-states, extending its posts along the mountains to the borders of Cashmere, so as to bear upon the left and rear of the enemy.

It must not, however, be forgotten, that if the banks of the Indus be selected as the most favourable position in which to expect the attack, the British troops will have an immense march to perform, in addition to the ill effect of exposure to the climate of the hotter parts of India for many months, if not years, before they are called to the conflict. If the European troops latest from England are made to replace those who have been longest in the country, whilst the latter proceed to the frontier, the field-force will contain none but seasoned men; but in that case, their freshness and energy will have been considerably impaired. From five to eight years are in all cases a sufficient seasoning for European troops in India. After that period, the effects of climate become speedily apparent on the constitutions of men possessing so little power or motive for restraint as common soldiers; they are no longer capable of enduring the fatigues and privations of protracted warfare; and one, or at most, two active campaigns, would be sufficient to exhaust their strength. We too easily allow ourselves to be deceived on this point, by the imposing accounts which are so often given of our Indian wars; and we fancy that, because our countrymen cheerfully undergo the labours of a campaign or two, they would be a match for any troops that could make their appearance upon the same theatre. These campaigns, however, have generally been fought within a short distance of our resources, and with all the conveniences and accommodations at hand, which old and undisturbed establishments can command, in a country entirely at the disposal of the service. In the few instances in which this has not been the case, we uniformly observe sickness to prevail amongst the European troops to an alarming extent; whilst the natives, if they suffer less from that cause, (which, however, is not always the fact,) suffer more from disaffection and desertion. So much, indeed, are the sepoys accustomed to make war within the boundaries of Hindostan alone, and in the comparatively easy mode alluded to, that they soon become disgusted with any service that threatens either to abridge their comforts, or to prolong their absence from their native plains. Of the three distinct armies which are at the disposal of the Indian Government, those of Madras and Bombay are generally considered to be better adapted for hard service than the Bengal troops; but as this is supposed to proceed entirely from the great attention which is paid to their equipment, and to the regular supply of every thing conducive to their comfort, when on foreign service, whilst the Bengal troops are in a great measure left to their own resources, it seems to follow, not only that the former are more expensive to the state, but that it will be difficult to bring large bodies of them to act with Bengal sepoys with reciprocal confidence and cordiality, without putting the latter upon an equality with them, in respect to pay, and all other advantages. Here, then, is another point to be attended to in conducting the defence of the country; and in order to secure an army which may act with union and effect, an equalization, in the particulars just referred to, of the troops of the three Presidencies, should immediately be adopted, upon the scale afforded by the most liberal of the whole.

But this is not all; in an army for the defence of India, assembled in the Punjab, comprising a considerable force of European as well as native troops, the former, though a great proportion of them would probably be over-seasoned, if brought up by easy marches, would benefit by the change of climate; whilst upon the latter, the cold and fatigue would have a directly contrary effect; and if harassed by active operations, especially night attacks, accompanied by that uncertainty of supplies which is likely to occur on such occasions, their number would shortly be diminished both by sickness and desertion, and a depression of spirits peculiar to the Hindoos, and resembling the *maladie du pays*, would unfit those who yet stood to their colours for any but the most ordinary camp duties. Under these circumstances, the Commander-in-Chief could never place entire reliance on the apparent strength of his army, as shown in figured statements; for although the natives would probably improve, if stationed nearer their own country, the Europeans would fall off in proportion to their exposure to the relaxing climate of Hindostan. Neither would the customs and institutions of the service be favourable to the views of the Commander; and there is reason to believe, that the peculiarities which appear to adapt an Indian army to the performance of the duties which are now entrusted to it, would, in some measure, incapacitate it for a conflict,* in comparison of

* The following description of the Russian soldiers will be read with deep interest by military men in India, as exhibiting the picture of an army admirably adapted for distant and arduous enterprises, even in a tropical climate:—"The Russian soldiers, unexcited by any spirituous liquors, with which the troops of other nations are often treated, previous to engaging in battle, make the sign of the cross, and, immovably fixing their eyes on their leader, follow him in the most profound silence—unanimous in their impetuosity, constant and imperturbable in danger—qualities which in military nations are the exclusive patrimony of perfect discipline. Frugal and patient under privations, as they are submissive, they spend the whole day in battle, and at night a ration of bread or biscuit, and a draught of water from the nearest brook, suffice to allay their hunger and thirst, whilst the bare ground for a bed, and their knapsack for a pillow, relieve their fatigue."—*Narrative of Don Juan Van Halen*, &c.

For a description of the Cossacks, too long to insert here, see Sir W. Scott's Life of Napoleon, vol. 5, p. 363.

which any service it has yet seen may be denominated mere "playing at soldiers."

The strength of the Company's army, includ-

The account of the Russian army, given by Sir Walter Scott, is also subjoined, as peculiarly interesting at the present moment:—"In the mode of disciplining their forces, the Russians proceeded on the system most approved in Europe. Their infantry was confessedly excellent, composed of men in the prime of life, and carefully selected as best qualified for military service. Their artillery was of the first description, so far as the men, guns and carriages, and appointments were concerned; but the rank of General of Artillery had not the predominant weight in the Russian army, which ought to be possessed by those particularly dedicated to the direction of that arm, by which, according to Napoleon, modern battles must be usually decided. The direction of their guns was too often entrusted to general officers of the line. The service of cavalry is less natural to the Russians than that of the infantry; but their horse regiments are nevertheless excellently trained, and have uniformly behaved well. But the Cossacks are a species of force belonging to Russia exclusively. The natives of the Don and the Volga hold their lands by military service, and enjoy certain immunities and prescriptions; in consequence of which, each individual is obliged to serve four years in the Russian armies. They are trained from early childhood to the use of the lance and sword, and familiarized to the management of a horse peculiar to the country, far from handsome in appearance, but tractable, hardy, swift, and sure-footed, beyond any breed perhaps in the world. At home, and with his family and children, the Cossack is kind, gentle, generous, and simple; but when in arms, and in a

ing the regiments of His Majesty's service usually stationed upon the continent of India, is about two hundred thousand upon the war establishment, exclusive of irregular corps of cavalry and infantry,

foreign country, he resumes the predatory, and sometimes the ferocious habits of his ancestors, the roving Scythians. As the Cossacks receive no pay, plunder is generally their object; and as prisoners were esteemed a useless incumbrance, they granted no quarter, until Alexander promised a ducat for every Frenchman whom they brought in alive. In the actual field of battle their mode of attack is singular. Instead of acting in line, a body of Cossacks about to charge, disperse at the word of command, very much in the manner of a fan suddenly flung open, and joining in a loud yell, or *hourra*, rush, each acting individually, upon the object of attack, whether infantry, cavalry, or artillery, to all of which they have been, in their wild way of fighting, formidable assailants. But it is as light cavalry that the Cossacks are, perhaps, unrivalled. They and their horses have been known to march one hundred miles in twenty-four hours without halting. They plunge into woods, swim rivers, thread passes, cross deep morasses, and penetrate through deserts of snow, without undergoing material loss, or suffering from fatigue. No Russian army, with a large body of Cossacks in front, can be liable to surprise; nor, on the other hand, can an enemy, surrounded by them, ever be confident against it. In covering the retreat of their own army, their velocity, activity, and courage, render pursuit by the enemy's cavalry peculiarly dangerous; and in pursuing a flying enemy, these qualities are still more redoubtable."—*Life of Napoleon Bonaparte*, vol. 5, p. 362, &c.

of which the latter are generally employed as guards and police in aid of the civil magistrates. In speaking of the defence of India, it is not unfrequently supposed that the whole of this force would be marshalled to oppose the invader on his crossing the Indus; but a very slight glance at the map will be sufficient to explain the absurdity of this expectation. The distance from Madras to the centre of the Punjab, is as great as that from Moscow to Paris; and from Calcutta to the same point, it is farther than from Madrid to Vienna. With such immense tracts of country in the rear of our army, tracts which are inhabited by various nations, differing as much from each other as the Portuguese from the Poles, it would be madness to attempt to concentrate more than a small proportion of the whole force upon a spot so far removed from the heart of our provinces. In point of fact, the greatest number of troops assembled for any one purpose in India, or upon any line of operations, has never been as much as fifty thousand. The regular forces at Seringapatam, though consisting of detachments from all the Presidencies, were less than forty thousand. The army before Burtpore, in 1825, did not amount to thirty thousand; and the whole of the regular Bengal forces assembled by Lord Hastings, either against the Nepaulese, or in his more extensive operations against the Pindarries and Mahrattas, did not much exceed forty thousand. The Bengal troops *employed* on the latter occasion were about fifty-five thousand, including irregular levies of all descriptions; these, however, were acting on a widely extended circle of concentric operations, and the army of occupation of each district contiguous to the seat of war, did not advance much beyond its accustomed boundary. On a straight line of operation towards the Indus, the case would be very different, and whole districts would be entirely denuded of troops. It is evident, then, that in the event of an invasion by a large army, the protecting force must either consist in a great measure of new levies, in addition to the present army of occupation, or new levies must be distributed about the provinces, in order to admit of the troops now stationed there being disposable. If we estimate the invading force at only fifty thousand men, it would require an equal force to defend the frontier, together with a strong reserve to form a rallying point, keep up the communication, and garrison the fortified places. The whole would not fall short of a hundred thousand men; and allowing only one fourth part of the number to be Europeans, we should have seventy-five thousand natives, either to be brought to the scene of action by long and toilsome marches from the remotest provinces, and through climates differing amongst each other as much as Spain and Italy do from Holland and Germany—or this portion of the army would be principally composed of new levies, drawn from the vicinity of the upper provinces, where the people, from circumstances which will be explained hereafter, are by no means well affected to the present government. Supposing, therefore, the Europeans to suffer nothing, either from the sudden change of climate, if arriving direct from England, or from being over-seasoned by the effects of a protracted residence in India, still, as they would have to bear the brunt of the attack against an army flushed with conquest, inured to fatigues, and allured by the hopes of plunder, their situation would be a very arduous one; for it is unreasonable to expect that our native troops, got together by either of the modes above described, would be a match for their opponents in the field, allowing three-fourths of the latter to be Persians, Affgans, or Tartars, disciplined in the Russian manner, or rather, intermixed in the same ranks with the Russian soldiers. Amidst the manifest disadvantages under which an army so circumstanced would labour, it would require the most consummate skill, on the part of the British commander, to conduct the most ordinary operations, even in the Punjab, where the face of the country is such as to afford positions favourable for defensive operations; but should the seat of war be transferred to Upper Hindostan, the whole tract lying between the Setledge and the richest part of the Bengal provinces, is so totally destitute of natural strength, that he would be unable to avoid coming to a general engagement in any other manner than by taking post under the walls of Delhi or Agra, and allowing the enemy to levy contributions on all the open country. The officers of the Company's service, it is true, have a perfect knowledge of the country, and are, perhaps, more accustomed to the management of large masses, than officers of corresponding rank in most other services; but on ground so perfectly level as that upon which they would have to manœuvre, those qualifications would be of very little assistance against an active and enterprising opponent, who, if inferior to themselves in those respects, would probably excel them in general military combination. But even on this point a good deal of exaggeration has been indulged in; and although the English would appear, if we judge from the accounts of battles gained and operations undertaken, to have waged war on a large scale in India, yet, as has been before remarked, their armies have always been comparatively small;

and they have been indebted for their triumphs to their skill and discipline having been so vastly superior to their opponents, and not to their numbers. There is no doubt, that the masses which they are in the habit of directing—though, agreeably to the usual proportion in Indian armies, not more than one-tenth consist of fighting-men, the rest being composed of baggage-servants and camp-followers,—have the effect of giving them the military *coup-d'œil*, and of training them to those habits of self-possession and command, which qualify them for entering upon a wider sphere of action, with less preparation than officers accustomed to the command of but very limited numbers; but this circumstance, though undoubtedly it renders the approach of more active warfare less formidable than it otherwise might appear, does not entirely supersede the necessity for considerable experience in actual operations with opponents more entitled to respect than those with whom they have hitherto been in the habit of coping.

As it is highly probable, then, that war, under a new aspect, will ere long approach our Indian possessions, and that the collision of England and Russia on the plains of Hindostan may be considered inevitable, to attempt to avert the storm by intriguing in the Court of Persia, is merely to prescribe for symptoms, instead of grappling with the disease itself. In place of employing every effort to conciliate the Persians, and to persuade them to adopt improvements in war and government, alike unsuited to the genius of the nation, and to the inclination of the leading families, we should turn our attention exclusively to our Indian empire, and take advantage of our unlimited influence and authority, to strengthen it, by infusing a feeling of love and respect for the British name, and a firm reliance on the mildness and the justice of its sway. A foreign government, ruling over such extensive realms as those now under the dominion of the Company, must have much more to apprehend from internal discontent, than from external force; and, in point of fact, we find that, since the Mussulman conquest, the invasion of Hindostan has not unfrequently been effected, by armies of comparatively inconsiderable strength, under a promise or expectation of support from the various tribes with which it is peopled,—tribes which all writers concur in describing as ever ready to rise in favour of the most formidable candidate for sovereign power. Baber states his army, enumerated too with apparent accuracy, to have amounted, great and small, good and bad, servants and no servants, to only twelve thousand men.—Memoirs, p. 293; and again, p. 310, "When

I invaded the country for the fifth time, overthrew Sultan Ibrahim, and subdued the empire of Hindostan, I had a larger army than I had ever before brought into it. My servants, the merchants, and their servants, and the followers of all descriptions that were in camp along with me, were numbered, and amounted to twelve thousand men." Nadir Shah, invited into Hindostan by some discontented nobles, defeated the imperial army with his advanced-guard alone; and when Ahmed Shah, better known by the name of Abdallah, was repulsed in his first attack upon Hindostan, the circumstance was attributed to his having neglected to secure the co-operation of any of the powerful tribes. The Tartars and Persians, then in the service of the Mogul, were a sufficient match for his army: on his second advance, however, being assured of the assistance of Gazi-ud-dein, at the head of the Tartar interest, he conquered Delhi without any difficulty; and in his subsequent expeditions always maintained the ascendency thus acquired. It is impossible, indeed, to peruse the history of the events just referred to, without being struck with the apparent ease with which Hindostan may be invaded either from Cabul or Candahar. The nearest road from Herat to Cabul and Attoc, through Huzarah and the hills, though difficult, and at some seasons almost impassable, is only a month's journey in fair weather; whilst the route by Candahar is described as straight and level, practicable without risk or trouble even in the winter, and requiring about forty or fifty days' march. If, however, Cabul be avoided, and the advance conducted through Candahar to Derah-Gazee-Khan, on the Indus, (the point at which the Affgans crossed that river, in their march to Cashmere, in 1813,) it would require only fifty or sixty days' march to bring an army from the centre of Khorasan to the rear of the Punjab, upon the very borders of the British territory.*

Under the bare possibility of such an event occurring, it would be interesting to ascertain the actual state of our frontier provinces in respect to

* It may be important to remark, that by whatever route the invasion of India by the Russians be accomplished, they will march with the stream of national antipathies in their favour—the Usbecs have a rooted hatred against the Persians, and rival the latter in their hostile feelings towards the Affgans; whilst the Affgans cherish as much resentment against the Seiks for their uninterrupted encroachments, as the Seiks do against the English, for protecting the apostate chiefs on the left bank of the Setledge. Should the invaders cross the Indus at Derah-Gazee-Khan, they might conciliate Runjeet Sing, the present ruler of the Punjab, and induce him to co-operate in an attack upon the Company's territories.

military preparation and local resources. Into this subject, however, it is not the intention of these pages to enter very deeply at present; but it may not be without its use to remark, that such is the security or supineness of the Indian Government, that, during the late siege of Burtpore, when the battering guns were fast becoming unserviceable from incessant firing, the nearest depôt, which was that of Agra, (from its situation and strength one of the most important stations in Upper India,) was incompetent to the supply of the requisite number to replace them. If the assault had failed, the army must have suspended its operations till both artillery and ammunition could have been procured from Allahabad, a distance of at least thirty days' march. This, too, it must be observed, was not in a part of the country where such an occurrence as a siege was unlooked for, but where the feeling of jealousy, which our failure in 1805 had occasioned, rendered the last twenty years little more than a season of preparation. In answer to this, it is asserted by the advocates of procrastination, that no serious intention to invade our north-western provinces could be manifested by the Russian Court, without affording us ample time for every species of preparation for defence. But, in addition to the example just given, it should be remembered, that the war with Ava, though for years considered unavoidable, yet found the Indian Government almost entirely unprepared; so much so, indeed, that it cannot be denied, that if the Burmese general, Maha Bundoolah, had boldly pushed forward, after the decisive affair at Ramoo, he would have met with little or no opposition in his advance upon Chittagong and Dacca, and might even have insulted the very suburbs of Calcutta. The north-western frontier, indeed, has been attended to more than any other, as the course of events has naturally led to that result; but it is doubtful whether, at the present moment, the whole country above Allahabad contain the necessary equipments for an army of fifty thousand men. Neither is it certain that the whole of the Company's provinces could furnish a remount* of suit-

* In Bengal, the government stud may be calculated to contain about six or seven thousand brood-mares—the upper, or northern division, however, has not yet been productive; and the whole taken together have not hitherto been adequate to the supply of horses for the horse-artillery and dragoons, without taking the native cavalry into the account. The dispersion of the Pindarries transferred a number of mares to the Company's provinces; but breeding was not much attended to until of late years, when entire horses being imported from Europe, Government formed the northern division of the stud out of those materials. It requires, however, the greatest vigilance, on the part of the inspectors, to prevent the admission of undersized or defective

able horses for the cavalry and horse-artillery, or cattle for the provision and transport of so large an army beyond two campaigns. The habits of the

animals; and on this account the annual produce of serviceable horses is by no means commensurate with the expense to the state. Indeed, the territorial system of the Company so greatly augments the value of land hitherto appropriated to pasturage, that breeding upon a large scale seems to require the encouragement of very high prices for horses, and it may perhaps be doubted whether cattle of all kinds be not upon the decrease throughout the provinces. The Seik Rajah, with the short-sighted policy common to semi-barbarous states, has lately opposed, to the utmost of his power, the importation of horses into the Company's territories, through his dominions, from the north; which has ever been the principal mart, as the indigenous supply of Hindostan has at all times been small. In acting in this manner, however, he has rendered us no inconsiderable service, by turning the attention of the Indian Government to the necessity of improving their internal resources. But establishments for this purpose, when in the hands of Government, are more expensive and less productive than when left to private speculation; yet, in Hindostan, the pressure of taxation is so great, and accumulation is so completely checked, that few individuals possess the means of entering upon a business which requires so large an outlay, and the returns of which are so precarious. The horses bred in this manner, without the assistance of Government, are now scarcely more than sufficient for the supply of the irregular cavalry, in which corps the troopers themselves, or their immediate commanders, contract for the horses. In the Madras territory, since the abolition of the Ganjam stud, there has been no breeding district, excepting on a very

people are not such as to lead them to rear any but the small breed of cattle commonly used for purposes of agriculture and traffic, and for the

limited scale by private dealers: the celebrated Manantoddy jungle has almost ceased to afford any considerable number, and the remains of the breed from which the Mysorean horse were furnished, are fast disappearing, notwithstanding a feeble attempt lately made to encourage them. The practice, indeed, both at Madras and Bombay, of importing horses for the service of Government, as well as for private purposes, from Arabia and Persia, tends greatly to depress the country market.

In Bombay, according to Mr. Chaplin's statement, there were in the whole Company's territories, in 1824, probably not more than 6000 horses, and of these, but a small number of description whose progeny would answer for the service of our cavalry.

If, therefore, the importation of horses from Persia and Arabia were to cease, or be materially affected, as would probably be the case if the Russians were to establish an influence in the Court of the Shah, it is not difficult to foresee what would be the embarrassment occasioned to our army. A complete remount for the regular cavalry, including dragoons and horse-artillery, of the three Establishments, would require about thirty thousand horses, besides the smaller description required for the foot-artillery and irregular corps. The march of cavalry and artillery from remote stations to the seat of war, would alone expend more than could well be replaced at the present moment, even by the the liberality of the King of Oude, (who has before now mounted regiments of dragoons,) or by the expensive markets of carriage-cattle to be found at Calcutta, Madras, and Bombay.

dairy; and the breed of ponies called Tattoos, for general purposes. Extensive requisitions could only be complied with at the expense of the growing harvest, or of a serious interruption of the ordinary occupation of the inhabitants. Our army would be under the necessity of carrying its supplies of all kinds in its train, or otherwise it would prove as great a scourge to our own territories as the most rapacious invader; and in the event of a reverse, instead of falling back upon its resources, it would have to continue its retreat through an exhausted, and probably an exasperated population.

When hostilities commenced with Ava, the greater part of the expedition to Rangoon and Arracan was supplied from the Madras Presidency; Bengal was exempted from any considerable demands either for men, or for cattle and stores; and yet, although the declaration of war was issued in February 1824, supplies for the advance of a force through Cachar to Ava, had not been collected in September of the same year; and when that expedition was given up, and a much smaller one, under General Morrison, ordered to proceed, by Chittagong to Arracan, it was not till January 1825, that the troops were able to advance, and that with only a portion of their stores and cattle. Now, if this was the case with an army of six or seven thousand, marching in the neighbourhood of our capital, and through some of the most rich and densely populous of our provinces, with the streams of the great rivers favourable for the transport of supplies of all kinds; what are we to expect when all these conditions are reversed? when supplies have to mount the long and often difficult course of the Ganges and Jumna against a powerful current; where the country is comparatively wild and unproductive; where the inhabitants are, from recent conquest and other causes, by no means well affected to the Government; and when they will be called upon for supplies, not for a mere detachment, but for an army perhaps a hundred thousand strong?

In speaking of supplies being sent to the Upper Provinces, it should be mentioned, that although the Company's territory, on the Bengal establishment, is remarkably deficient in good roads fit for military purposes,—the great rivers, in fact, affording a comparatively economical means of communication from Calcutta to Furrackabad and Delhi,—there is no public establishment of boats or river craft for the conveyance of stores. When supplies of any kind are required in the field stations, boats are hired by the army commissariat, ostensibly at a small expense, but in reality at a very great one; for such is the defective state of those which alone are procurable for the public service, and so badly are they navigated, that the accidents which occur in the loss of men, as well as stores, would form a very serious addition to the general rate of transport. The actual cost, also, is materially enhanced by the slow mode of travelling, and the difficulty of conducting a fleet of boats to such immense distances by means of the track-rope. From forty to sixty are as many as can be taken by one opportunity, according to the system now in force; and these, conveying altogether not more than twelve hundred tons upon an average, are three months in reaching Allahabad, and from thence two to Agra, and one to Futtighur; from either of which points, it would require a march of thirty days to reach the banks of the Setledge. When, indeed, we consider the difficulty of collecting transport, the slow rate of travelling against the strong current of the Ganges, and the limited supply either of stores or men which each fleet can convey, it is perhaps not too much to assert, that supposing the Russians to have secured, by treaty or otherwise, a free passage through Persia, they could at any time collect an army of fifty or a hundred thousand men upon the banks of the Indus, as soon as, and perhaps sooner, than the Indian Government could complete the necessary arrangements for opposing them with effect. Startling as this opinion may appear, it is only necessary to consult the map, and to bear in mind the ease with which Russia can accumulate troops of all descriptions in her south-eastern frontier, to demonstrate its possible correctness. If Russia were, immediately after declaring war, to direct her attention to this point, her army in Georgia would have been on its march long ere intelligence from Europe could reach Bengal. From the banks of the Kur (though it is probable the Russian boundary has already been pushed two hundred miles more to the south) to Herat, is about eleven hundred miles, or one hundred and ten days' march; and from Herat to the Indus at Cabul, or at Derah-Gazee-Khan, as has been already stated, is about fifty days' march, making upon the whole one hundred and sixty marches. Now, if we may believe the published Army Lists, in the whole of the territory above Allahabad, including Oude, Rohilcund, and Rajhpootanah, there are not more than* forty-five

* To these may be added such troops as the Bombay Presidency could spare: but, in this case, the march from Mhow, Guzerat, and Cutch, to Moultan, or to Loodianah, on the Setledge, would be somewhat greater than from Allahabad to the last mentioned place; with the disadvantage of having a country but partially known, and certainly but badly supplied with necessaries of all kinds for troops to

thousand regular troops, including the regiments of His Majesty's service; and of these only about twenty thousand are nearer the frontier than twenty marches. But as no advance into the Punjab could prudently be attempted with less than thirty thousand men, it would be necessary to draw troops from stations as distant as Allahabad, which is at least fifty days' march from the frontier. So far, however, there appears to be a great difference in favour of the Indian army reaching the point of rendezvous before the assailants; but we are not to overlook the important consideration, that of all the troops thus collected together, only about seven thousand five hundred are Europeans. To provide the necessary escorts and communications, and to raise the European force to the number of twenty thousand—which may be looked upon as the smallest proportion, if the invaders should cross the Indus with fifty thousand men—troops would have to march from all parts of our provinces, from a distance of twelve and fifteen hundred miles, proceeding either

pass through. A division from Bombay, however, would be of the greatest service in threatening the right flank of the invading army, and in operating upon his communications, in the event of his pushing on to Delhi; though the moral effect, upon the natives, of his gaining possession of that capital, would render it a matter of the utmost consequence to oppose him, before he could advance so far.

by the course of the rivers, or across a country but very indifferently provided either with roads or with the requisite supplies for such a force; and it would be necessary to send to Ceylon, the Mauritius, and even the Cape of Good Hope, for regiments of His Majesty's service to supply the place of those sent to the frontier.

Upon the whole, then, if we attend to the events now passing in Persia, and consider the great probability that Russia will ere long establish a permanent influence in that kingdom, too much attention cannot be paid to the political strength of our Indian provinces; and whatever may be the assistance which we can expect from the spirit or patriotism of the inhabitants, no time should be lost in providing those safeguards, which, as the conquerors of that extensive region, we are bound, as well in justice, as from a regard to our own welfare, to afford. But in order to estimate the degree of attachment which the Indian Government can claim, it will now be necessary to take a view of the condition of the people submitted to its sway.

Since the foregoing pages were written, advice has been received that, in consequence, no doubt, of the diversion which the increasing importance of the affairs of Greece has operated in favour of

Persia, Russia has made peace with that power. The conditions are severe; and while they secure to Russia at all times an easy access to Tabriz and Teheran, they put her in possession of a sum of money not only sufficient to defray the expense of the late war, but to provide means of future aggression, whenever it may suit her to renew hostilities. The war, indeed, may be considered to have set at rest the question, as to the practicability of transporting a large army from Russia to the heart of Persia: not only has the feeble barrier of the Araxes been passed, but the disposition of the inhabitants of the contiguous provinces to assist an invader, ascertained beyond all doubt. With little or no apparent effort on the part of Russia, a large and well-equipped army was assembled to the south of the Caucasus, and put in motion upon the capital of Persia, without the latter being able to offer any effectual resistance, or, indeed, possessing any other means of saving her hoarded treasures, than the immediate sacrifice of a considerable portion of them, at the discretion of the conqueror. Such, too, is acknowledged to be the state of anarchy and disorder in which the greater part of Persia is plunged, that the Shah is fearful of removing the remains of his treasure to a more distant asylum; whilst, therefore, his known avarice is a sufficient guarantee against profusion, the immense hoardings, which, according to a late writer, will amount to nearly thirty millions sterling, when the present demand has been satisfied,* will still be within the reach of Russia on any future occasion. On the other hand, the Shah's advanced age and growing infirmities render it not improbable that Russia may very shortly be appealed to, to settle the claims of rival candidates for the throne; in which case the devotion of Jehangir Khan, the present governor of Ardebil, to the cause of Russia, will no doubt meet with its reward, in the recognition of his relationship to the legitimate royal stock of Persia, for the assertion of which, his father was cruelly put to death by the present Shah. The present Prince Royal, Abbas Mirza, has rendered himself unpopular in the north-western provinces, by his arbitrary conduct during the progress of hostilities; and has lost the confidence of the nation, no less by the manner in which he forced the kingdom into a war, than by the rash and inconsiderate manner in which he opposed the advance of the enemy's force. Little doubt, therefore, need be entertained that in the event of peace with Constantinople again setting the southern division of the Russian forces at liberty,

* See Lieut. Alexander's Travels.

the late designs upon Persia will be resumed, and ample advantage taken of the information now acquired respecting the deficiencies, moral and physical, under which that unfortunate country appears destined to labour.

But whatever may be the future views of our great Northern rival, the respite which has thus been afforded to the Indian Government is most valuable. Had the Russians continued to advance, the alarm which had begun to pervade our frontier provinces would have so greatly encreased, as, in some measure, to have impaired the character of any measure which might be adopted for improving the condition of the inhabitants of that part of our territory, by giving it the appearance of being rather extorted by our fears than conceded by our justice. Now, however, all immediate danger being removed, and the recurrence, though still within the bounds of probability, not impossibly distant in point of time, no such motives can be inferred. Indeed the only apprehension now is, that the improvidence of the Governors will lead them to neglect the solemn warning which they have received, and induce them again to consider the governed as safe from attack,* and as firm in their allegiance, as if no

* Symptoms of this have already appeared in the orders issued respecting the reduction of the army:—from ten to

such danger had ever offered itself, or as if they had not just reason to complain of the general impoverishment to which they are reduced.

twenty men per company in the infantry, and the same in the cavalry, have been reduced, and some companies of artillery have been dismounted and the horses sold. The impolicy of this proceeding, respecting the cavalry and artillery in particular, must be manifest from what has been observed with regard to the scarcity of horses in India; and the demand being so greatly reduced, there will be little or no encouragement for breeding; and, in addition to the time required for properly breaking horses for the public service, Government will not be able to procure them in the event of a sudden call. Advantage should be taken of a period of peace to prepare ourselves in every point for future wars; and if retrenchment in expenditure must be made, it should only be in those departments which admit of being easily restored to their original strength in time of need.

# CHAPTER III.

## ON THE CONDITION OF THE PEOPLE OF HINDOSTAN.

> "Verum illi (nostri majores) delubra deorum pietate, domos suas gloriâ decorabant; neque victis quidquam, præter injuriæ licentiam, eripiebant. At hi contrâ, ignavissimi homines per summum scelus, omnia ea sociis adimere, quæ fortissimi viri victores hostibus reliquerunt: proinde quasi injuriam facere, id demum esset imperio uti."

In the last chapter, it has been shown that the defence of India against the attacks of a really formidable power would require not only a more efficient army than that which is now distributed throughout its provinces, but that even the best organized force would find it difficult to subsist itself in any part of the country without being as detrimental to its prosperity as if it were on hostile ground. With the exception of a few tribes, not very respectable as to numbers, we have perhaps little to apprehend from the open assistance which the people of the country might be disposed to afford the common enemy; but even their lukewarmness, their indifference to the fate of the present Government, would be pregnant with the most disastrous consequences. If, indeed, it be doubted whether any country can be conquered when its inhabitants resolve to be free, it must follow that no foreign occupant can successfully defend it, unless the inhabitants range themselves unequivocally on his side. It is, therefore, of the first importance, to endeavour to ascertain the actual condition of the people, and what is their attachment to the soil they cultivate, and to the government under which they live.

The habits of the Mohammedan conquerors of Hindostan leading them to indulge in pomp and sensuality, the love of ease and pleasure soon influenced their demeanour towards the vanquished; and if the feelings as well as the interests of the Hindoos were generally disregarded, they at least derived some consolation from seeing their fellow-countrymen occasionally raised to high dignity and power, both in the civil and military departments of the state. It is true that this was too frequently the consequence of forced alliance and polluted blood; but the patient idolater, as soon as the sense of personal degradation was overcome, did not disdain to profit himself and his kindred by the influence thus obtained. On the other hand, if wealth to an enormous amount was wrested from them, often under circumstances of the greatest cruelty, still that wealth was dissipated as freely as it was obtained, and the greater part of it flowed back in refreshing streams upon the industry of the country. It may be remarked, too, that the Mohammedans, though differing as much as Christians do, in religion, from the Hindoos, were yet of the same flesh and blood; in the great family of nature they were kindred; and the same sun that shed its genial influence upon the one, cheered and animated the other. But with the English every thing is different: the climate of India is looked upon as foreign and ungenial; to them the country is forbidden ground; they are only allowed to reside in it as sojourners anxious to regain their native homes; and whilst their exactions surpass those of all former rulers, they individually support a smaller expenditure than the natives can be induced to believe is consistent with the stations they hold, and the wealth appropriated to their support. With every allowance for variation of national character, their expenditure in India is, generally speaking, on the lowest scale of decent subsistence, according to their several ranks; their surplus income is remitted to Europe, and they, as well as their employers, appear to look upon

Hindostan as a patrimony granted to them for the support of their families on the other side of the globe. Almost the whole of what is wrung from the people, ostensibly in requital for the protection afforded them by the Government, instead of being laid out in *bona fide* state expenditure, for the advantage of the country, is devoted to the payment of the interest of debts contracted by the Company in their character of merchants, and in the past or present support of foreign establishments, such as Prince of Wales's Island, Bencoolen, and St. Helena, maintained avowedly for commercial purposes. Add to this the depression of the higher classes, (which was the unexpected consequence of the territorial system of revenue,) and their exclusion from places of trust and emolument,—the little employment given to the natives in general, in consequence of the economical scale of our Indian establishments —and the small number of our troops compared with the countless multitudes of an armed force constituted according to Asiatic notions of parade and splendour; and we may easily comprehend how infinitely more severely our Christian rule must bear upon the condition and prosperity of the people, than that of any previous conqueror. It is to this account that we should have to place the apathy of the inhabitants in the event of any serious danger threatening the Anglo-Indian Government:—the impoverishment of the country might not be revenged upon us in deeds of insurrection and blood, but theirs would be the *vox silentio tenuis*, which, though not heard in the whirlwind or in the earthquake, would speak dismay and ruin to the hearts of their oppressors; and the reckless indifference with which they would behold the struggle, even if they abstained from open hostility, would be decisive of the fate of their present rulers; for no army ever yet withstood the energies of a powerful invading foe, if unsupported by the sympathy of the country which it was endeavouring to defend.

From what has been before remarked respecting the territorial acquisitions of the Company, it will readily be conceived that nothing could have been less calculated to encourage the expectation of any improvement in the condition of the people, than the principle of actual pecuniary profit upon which those acquisitions were made. Without pausing to reflect that the several powers then holding possessions in India, if not in open rebellion against their legitimate sovereign, were certainly foreigners and intruders on the soil, whole tracts and provinces were accepted as gifts, or conquered by force of arms, as if the aboriginal inhabitants were not more worthy of consideration than the trees and other productions to be found on the surface. According to the barbarous computation of oriental despots, countries were only valuable in proportion to the direct land revenue they yielded; the happiness of the inhabitants never entered into the calculation; and the slow and often interrupted progress of arts and commerce afforded no other available source of income. The occurrence of wars and revolutions rarely permitted any hope of improvement in the amount; and as amidst the scenes of pillage that took place under a system of graduated plunder, from the prince down to the smallest functionary, every thing was destroyed or dissipated that came within the reach of man,—the land, which appeared to be the only indestructible element of production, came to be considered as the sole property of the ruler. It was of this principle, which in itself exhibited the very essence of anarchy, ignorance, and misrule, that a Christian establishment, emanating from a community in which civilization and refinement were supposed to have attained their highest point, were not ashamed to avail themselves. Following the worthy prototypes which the history of Asiatic barbarism and tyranny afforded them, the India Company declared that the farmer's dues were in effect those of the state; and subsequently, when, under the reforms introduced by Lord Cornwallis, they ostensibly bestowed proprietary rights upon the zemindars, they first appropriated to the state the whole produce of the soil, after paying the expenses of cultivation, and one-tenth of the rental to the newly created landholder. In addition, however, to Asiatic principles and precedents, and to the learning and research bestowed by Patton* to prove that the sovereign was sole proprietor, or, which amounts to the same thing, the *sole disposer* of landed property, arguments were not long undiscovered, whereby to confer on this principle the sanction of more competent authority; and Blackstone is quoted by one of the writers in support of the Company's prerogative to prove, that if a "subject in England has only the usufruct and not the absolute property in the soil—or, as Sir Edward Coke expresses it, he has *dominium utile*, but not *dominium directum*—a ryot in India may rest contented with an usufructuary right." But, besides that this principle in the law of England—resting as it does upon the doctrine of escheats, by which the sovereign of the state succeeds to all inheritance to which no other title can be found, and by which lands, like all other property, revert to and vest in the King, who in the eye of the law is the universal lord and original proprietor of all

* Principle of Asiatic Monarchies.

the land in his kingdom—is declared by Blackstone (2.50) to be, "in reality, a mere fiction;" it forms part only of that constitution by which the King is solemnly sworn to govern his people according to the statutes in Parliament agreed on; if, therefore, the ryot of India is bound to rest contented with the same title to his ground that a subject of England possesses, to make the analogy complete, a free constitution should be given, and the quota of land-tax to be paid should be settled by his representatives in Parliament assembled.

Nothing, in truth, could have been more idle than the whole controversy concerning the right of property in the soil of India: the natives, whose very subsistence depended upon the issue, were unable to take any part in the discussion; and it is quite evident that the will of Government, which was alone commensurate with its power, was the only rule by which it was determined. Arguing from a state of things which had been produced by ages of plunder and desolation, the East India Company saw that the only rational mode of restoring the prosperity of the country, would interfere with the pecuniary aid which their commercial embarrassments rendered necessary, besides compelling them to abstain from all attempts to increase their rents until order was restored, and with it the peaceful and industrious habits of the community. Their interest as traders was, in fact, incompatible with the real interest of territorial rulers, supposed to have a sympathy with the prosperity of the country. The financial difficulties in which the Company's Government had involved themselves, did not allow them the necessary leisure to take a just and magnanimous view of the great and interesting question which the wonderful course of events had submitted to their decision; and, unhappily, the great Council of the nation, and the ever-watchful eye of the British public, were too distant to admit of effectual interference to save the inhabitants of India from the continuance of a system, which, even under the more lenient sway of Mohammedan rulers, had plunged the greater part of them in hopeless poverty.

When, however, the India Company and their Government ordained a permanent settlement of the land revenue in 1793, there is no doubt that it was their intention to renounce all claim to the proprietorship of the land in favour of the zemindars; but in omitting exactly to define, in the first instance, the relative situation of zemindar and ryot, the door appears to have been left open to so many alterations and interferences on the part of Government, as in a great measure to have reduced the proprietary right to a mere name. The interests of the ryots being in direct opposition to those of the landholders, the latter were soon found complaining that, unless they were armed with power, as prompt to enforce payment from their renters, as Government had authorised the use of in regard to its own claims, it was impossible for them to discharge their engagements with punctuality. Notwithstanding this appeal, however, Government appear to have been sceptical as to the ill effects of the system, until its interests * were likely to be affected, by the farther progress of the evils complained of, exposing portions of the land sold to the hazard of a reduction in the rates of assessment. It then interfered for the protection of the zemindars; and a regulation was enacted, "for better enabling individuals to recover arrears of rent or revenue due to them," [the opening of the preamble to which is to the

* Much the same reasons were given by Timur for protecting his subjects from ruin; "for the ruin of the subject causeth the diminution of the Imperial treasures:" a passage upon which Mr. Patton (Principles of Asiatic Monarchies) makes the following observation:—"This intimate connexion between the interest of the Sovereign and the prosperity of the husbandman (the immediate tenant of Government), is the surest pledge of his security." Such were the opponents of the permanent settlement in Bengal!

following effect :—" Government not admitting of any delay in the payment of the public revenue receivable from the proprietors and farmers of land, justice requires that they should have the means of levying their rents and revenues with equal punctuality, and that the persons by whom they may be payable, whether under farmers, dependant talookdars, ryots, or others, should be enabled, in like manner, to realize the rents and revenue from which their engagements with the proprietors or farmers are to be made."] By this regulation, the delays which a defaulter was enabled to oppose to the distrainer in enforcing payment of arrears of rent or revenue, as far as the amount was realizable from his crops or his personal property, were avoided, and the distrainer allowed, under specified conditions, to put up the property of the defaulter for sale, and to cause it to be sold, to make good the deficiency; and, in some cases, to confine the defaulter until he discharged the claim against him, together with interest, at twelve per cent. Thus the protection afforded to the cultivators by the permanent settlement was in effect withdrawn, and the landholders had it again in their power to practise all those oppressions and arbitrary exactions, which it had been the object of that settlement to abolish for ever. " It became the interest of the zemindar," as is observed by Mr. Thackery on another occasion, " not to assist, but to ruin the ryot, that he might eject him from his right of occupancy, and put in some one else on a raised rent ;"—and such was his power in this respect, that the cultivators, unable to bear up against their renewed oppressions, were frequently induced to abscond, in order to avoid imprisonment, in addition to the forfeiture of their whole property. It was from the operation of these two causes—the efforts of the landholders, on the one hand, to retain their station, and, if possible, to raise their share of the rents ; and of the ryots, on the other, to secure a fair remuneration for their labour,—that justified the following appalling picture, drawn by the Collector of Midnapore, in February 1802. " They (the zemindars) all say, that such a harsh and oppressive system was never before resorted to in this country ; that the custom of imprisoning landholders for arrears of revenue was, in comparison, mild and indulgent to them ; that though it was no doubt the intention of Government to confer an important benefit on them by abolishing this custom, it has been found, by melancholy experience, that the system of sales and attachments, which has been substituted for it, has, in the course of a few years, reduced most of the great zemindars in Bengal to distress and beggary, and produced a greater change in the landed property of Bengal than has perhaps ever happened in the same space of time in any age or country, by the mere effect of internal regulations." Estates were everywhere sold for default of revenue; and the purchasers, who supplanted the first proprietors, being in their turn unable to support themselves under such a system, the land was sold and re-sold, until it at length fell into the possession of a set of men who were content to act merely as the receivers of the land-tax, without having any farther interest in their estates, or incurring any risk but that of losing their office. This was, in fact, the natural result of the anomalous position in which the zemindar was placed in respect to Government and to the ryots; responsible to the former for the whole amount assessed on his estate, and necessarily at the mercy of the latter, when the least delay in realizing that amount occasioned a sale of his property to make good the defalcation, he was gradually deprived of every thing he possessed, besides the tenth share of the rents, which formed his commission for collecting the whole. No individual thus circumstanced could be supposed to have the power, even if he had the will, to attend to the comforts and prosperity of his tenants; and whilst, for want of capital, no attempt could be made by the latter to improve their condition, without overwhelming them with debt, no subsequent effort could release them; because every advantage which was gained excited the covetousness of their landlord, and induced him to make use of all the means in his power to dispossess them, and procure a higher rent from their successor. This consideration operated as a complete bar to improvement; and, in fact, the only reasonable prospect which offered itself to such of the landholders as still possessed sufficient capital, was to turn their attention to the cultivation of such waste land as lay within the boundary of their estates, and the produce of which, agreeably to the spirit of the act of permanent settlement, was not liable to farther taxation.

In a climate like that of India, where vegetation is so rapid, and where inundations are so frequent, ground very soon runs to waste and becomes overgrown with brushwood. Colebrooke estimates the proportion of land tilled in Bengal and Behar at only one-third of the whole surface; and gives it as his opinion, in an extreme case, that a period of thirty years scarcely covers the barren sand with soil—when inundations have been caused, as sometimes occurs, by rivers breaking through their banks or changing their course. It requires, indeed, at all times, a considerable expense of money and labour to clear wastes that are overgrown with jungle; in most cases, two or three years must elapse before it is discovered how much of the ground, so cleared, will yield a sufficient remuneration; and if to these considerations be added the ill effects of poverty and ignorance, in persevering upon an exaggerated estimate of profit, some idea may be formed of the difficulty of reclaiming land under similar circumstances, and of the degree of encouragement which it would be desirable to hold out for such employment of capital. Instances, indeed, have not been wanting, of individuals having entirely ruined themselves, after a perseverance of upwards of twenty years, in their endeavour to reclaim waste lands in different parts of India. Fortunately, such instances are rare, but they serve to show the difficulty attending improvements of this nature. The Indian Government, however, still adhering to the principle, that all profits derived from the land are in effect those of the state, have not only allowed themselves to be prevailed upon, in consequence of this very partial improvement of the condition of the landholders, to withhold the benefits of a permanent settlement from the ceded and conquered provinces, although under the most solemn engagements to grant them, but they have endeavoured, and are still endeavouring, by a sort of *quo warranto* process, to assert their right to share in the augmentation of income, which some zemindars have procured at so much expense and hazard to themselves individually. In regard to the north-western provinces, in particular, nothing can be at once so unjust and so impolitic as such conduct. The whole population of that part of the country, which is most exposed to foreign aggression—a race of men well known to be more robust and more prone to military habits than in any other part of India—instead of being attached to the Government, by being attached to the soil, which they ought to protect, are kept in an unsettled and discontented condition; ready to believe that nothing but a change of masters can free them from the state of impoverishment in which they are plunged;—whilst the great landholders are deterred from attending to the happiness and prosperity of their tenantry, by the apprehension that Government will step in and appropriate all the profits, as they are thought to be doing in the rest of their dominions.

The effect of these circumstances in discouraging agriculture, it is unnecessary to insist upon; but the injury thus inflicted upon the country is greatly enhanced by the change which a few years have wrought in its commercial prospects. When British influence was first established in Bengal, the country was literally crowded with manufacturers and artisans of all descriptions. The various officers, both of the Mogul court and the subordinate principalities and governments, with their numerous retainers, occasioned an immense consumption of every article which luxury could desire, or the ingenuity of the country produce; and some of these, on account of their beauty and costliness, formed the basis of a considerable export trade. But on the substitution of a comparatively economical European Government, the demand for productions of this nature almost entirely ceased; the industry of the country everywhere met with a sensible check; and the finishing blow was put to many of those manufactures, for which India had been so long celebrated, by the fabrics of Europe being made to rival them in delicacy of workmanship, and even to surpass them in cheapness. Nothing was then reserved for the industry of the natives but such articles as were too coarse or too valueless to excite competition; and the great increase of the import trade soon converted India almost exclusively into a market for raw produce. This great revolution in the commercial interests of the country was calculated to arouse all the vigilance, and call for all the forbearance, of a Government which had the welfare of its subjects at heart. The great change which had taken place in the condition of the people, who, from being composed of a mass of manufacturing classes, sufficient to furnish ample employment for the agricultural class, became suddenly transformed into a nation of cultivators, called imperiously for the fostering hand of Government to increase and improve the produce of the soil, by the adoption of every expedient which industry, skill, and capital could apply to it, and to create such other employment as the nature, wants, and habits of the people would admit. In all countries where the great bulk of the inhabitants gain their subsistence by cultivating the soil, the natural increase of population will soon exceed the demand for employment, and the wages of labour will be gradually reduced to the lowest possible rate. Nothing can avert or even retard the general distress and misery consequent upon this state of things, but the extension and improvement of agriculture, the encouragement of industry to furnish employment to the surplus population, and the diffusion of education and intelligence; by the operation of which new wants and new tastes will be engendered sufficient to impart a stimulus to the industry and ingenuity of all classes. The Indian Government, however, as we have seen, acted upon diametrically opposite principles. When the amount of the land-tax had been fixed in perpetuity at a rate which there was every reason to suppose would drain the surplus earnings of the whole agricultural community into the coffers of the state, a permanent settlement with the ceded and conquered provinces, though distinctly promised under the governments of Lord Wellesley and Lord Minto, is withheld from time to time, in the hope of gradually enticing the landholders to make such improvement, as may afford an opportunity of approximating to the maximum assessment which the produce of the soil will admit; because, in a few instances, the landholders of Bengal and Behar have been able to accumulate more wealth than could reasonably have been anticipated. Nor is this indecent appetence of revenue confined to the regulations enacted of late years,—regulations which appear to be passed for no other purpose than to be subjects of perpetual discussion and illusive amendment—but it is made to apply retrospectively even to rights and privileges which existed before the acquisition of the Dewanny, and which had been recognised by every successive government; for the tenures by which certain lands have been held rent-free from time immemorial have come at length to be questioned, and many of them have lately been resumed, whilst others are, at this moment, under sequestration.

When the English first appeared upon the plains of India, there were so many native princes and chieftains in the exercise of sovereign power, and these personages were so easily induced to alienate their rights for the sake of immediate advantage, that it is probable the custom of granting lands rent-free continued even after the Company had unequivocally assumed political rule. It was necessary, therefore, to inquire into and put a stop to an abuse which threatened to make such serious inroads upon the fiscal jurisdiction of the state; and accordingly, as far back as 1783, a regulation was passed, that all rent-free land, in whatever quantity, unless held under the sanction of a grant from the Governor and Council, or unless possession thereof had been obtained antecedent to the Dewanny grant, were resumable. To this regulation no reasonable objection could be made; though such is reported to have been the number of claims for land which then called for confirmation, that it is supposed a very great portion of them was left unadjusted by the Committee empowered to carry the above resolution into effect.

These lands are chiefly of four descriptions,* the Devutter and Pirutter, granted for the endow-

* See Mr. Grant's Analysis of the Finances of Bengal, Fifth Report, Appendix, p. 290 and 318.

ment of Hindoo and Mohammedan temples, respectively; Bramutter, lands appropriated for the maintenance of Bramins; and Mohutran, or honorary grants to individuals. The two latter descriptions may be sold, or otherwise disposed of; but the two first are for ever devoted to the purposes for which they were originally granted; and an order of Government, on the occasion referred to, prohibited the granting of land for religious or charitable purposes in future without the express sanction of the state, though existing proprietors were confirmed in their possessions. Affairs remained in this situation for many years, but at length an order was issued, decreeing that rent-free lands should be resumed, unless the proprietors of them could produce their sunnuds, or grants, for the inspection of the Collector of the district; when those found to bear unequivocal marks of validity were to be confirmed, and the others rescinded.* As, however, much of the land

* By a subsequent regulation, rent-free land, not exceeding ten biggahs in extent (about 3 acres), are exempted from the operation of this decree, upon proof being produced of such lands having been in the possession of the family now holding them for a certain specified period. There is little doubt, however, that the revenue records which were deposited in the Khalsah when the permanent settlement was made, do actually contain the registry of most of the rent-free estates which are now about to be resumed.

in question had been granted many years, and in some cases centuries, before the establishment of the Company's Government, it was scarcely probable that sunnuds and titles could have been preserved, amidst the scenes of violence and commotion which had so frequently occurred; neither public nor private registers could be supposed to have survived the general wreck; though the known habits of the people were perfectly consistent with the belief that such property continued to descend in the families to which it had been originally given.

To these evils arising out of the extreme uncertainty of their rights, where every privilege is assumed to be held by sufferance, liable to the revision or resumption of Government, without even the form of open investigation, must be added the imposition of stamp-duties, bearing with peculiar severity upon the under tenants and cultivators, and which were a direct consequence of the act of permanent settlement.

The natives of India, but particularly the inhabitants of what are termed the Lower Provinces of the Bengal Presidency, cherish a very general and sincere veneration for the character of Lord Cornwallis; and with reason look upon him as the champion of their rights, and the founder of the few privileges which still remain to them. His professed desire to make their protection depend solely upon the laws, and not upon the individual character of their rulers; and his consequent separation of the financial from the judicial functions, and making public officers in the former department responsible for their conduct to the courts established in the principal cities and districts; his regulating courts of appeal and last resort; his abolition of judges' fees, as well as all other charges which set a price upon justice, and made it difficult of access in proportion to the poverty and helplessness of the suitor; his recommending and laying the foundation of a code of laws, laying down rules for the conduct of all, and specifying the mode of attaining speedy redress for every injury; and the care he took to explain the grounds of every regulation he enacted, and to appeal to the good sense of the people upon all subjects affecting their rights, persons, or property,—called for, and still command, their fervent admiration, and justly entitled that distinguished nobleman to the gratitude, not only of India, but of all mankind. Accustomed, as the natives of India are, to look up to their rulers with a deference and respect little short of adoration, they hailed with heartfelt gratitude these manifestations of a kind and beneficent mind; but in proportion to the sincerity of this feeling, is the dismay with which they have witnessed the almost total abrogation of measures, the reasons of which had been so fully and satisfactorily laid open to their understanding, and a system infinitely more severe and inflexible than any they had before seen, substituted in its place. Innumerable are the traditions current throughout the provinces, concerning the love of justice, and the strictly impartial mind, for which Lord Cornwallis was celebrated; they consider his regulations as having established and conveyed to them benefits till then unknown, or only existing in their legendary abstractions of what a perfect ruler should be. His equal administration of justice, by rules which professed to disregard the persons and qualities of men, and to be free from the influence of the Government itself, gained all their confidence; and if the land-tax appeared to be so great, as to leave the ostensible proprietor an inadequate share of the rents of his estate, still the amount taken was "fixed, and for ever," and admitted of relative diminution, by the effect of increased industry. This certainty of exemption from future demands, notwithstanding the disadvantage under which they laboured, in being in a great measure excluded from taking any part in the government of their country, and in being debarred from receiving assistance and instruction from the settlement of intelligent Europeans amongst them, still offered considerable inducement to them to improve their property by cultivating the more valuable articles of produce, and by clearing waste or uncultivated lands:—like the lever of Archimedes, industry only required ground to stand upon, to enable it to move the universe; and that ground they beheld in the security to persons and property, which it was his Lordship's anxious wish to establish.

It is singular, however, that although Lord Cornwallis successfully combated the reasons for delaying, for ten years, the final announcement of a permanent settlement, which Mr. Shore had adduced, he never appears to have entertained a doubt as to the prior right of the zemindars to the property of the soil. "Mr. Shore has most ably, and, in my opinion,"* observes his Lordship, "most successfully argued in favour of the rights of the zemindars to the property of the soil." But if the value of permanency is to be withdrawn from the settlement now in agitation, of what avail will the power of his arguments be to the zemindars, for whose rights he has contended? They are now to have their property in farm for a lease of ten years, provided they will pay as

* Fifth Report, Appendix, p. 473.

good a rent for it; and this property is then to be again assessed, at whatever rent the Government of this country may at that time think proper to impose. In any part of the world, where the value of property is known, would not such a concession of a right of property in the soil be called a cruel mockery?" The interest of the zemindar was, in point of fact, too intimately blended with the proprietary right to be easily separated; but nothing is more clear, throughout the whole controversy, than that the position which he occupied constituted a disturbing cause by which the plumb-line of justice, in making the proprietary recognition, was warped from the perpendicular, and the entire calculation affected with error accordingly. The ryot was the real proprietor—he paid the rent of the land to the zemindar as an agent of Government only. The zemindar was a civil officer of police, as well as revenue; he was bound to make good his stipulated payment of revenue, under penalty of suffering an equivalent loss of property, or of being deprived of the whole; it was his duty to preserve the peace of the country, and his services were required for the defence of the state, against rebellion or invasion, according to his means of furnishing that assistance. From all these duties, however, excepting the collection of the rents, our system of government relieved him; and, in principle, he had no farther right than that which the justice of Lord Cornwallis conceded to those who were likely to suffer from the resumption of the Sayer. "As to the question of right,"* observes his Lordship, "I cannot conceive that any Government in their senses would ever have delegated an authorised right to any of their subjects to impose arbitrary taxes on the internal commerce of the country. It certainly has been an abuse that has crept in, either through the negligence of the Mogul governors, who were careless and ignorant of all matters of trade; or, what is more probable, connivance of the Mussulman aumil, who tolerated the extortion of the zemindar, that he might again plunder him in his turn. But be that as it may, the right has been too long established, or tolerated, to allow a just Government to take it away without indemnifying the proprietor for the loss; and I never heard that, in the most free state, if an individual possessed a right that was incompatible with the public welfare, the legislature made any scruple of taking it from him, provided they gave him a fair equivalent. The case of the late Duke of Athol, who, a few years ago, parted very unwillingly with the sovereignty of the Isle of Man, appears to me to be exactly in point." The

* Fifth Report, Appendix, p. 475.

situation of the zemindars bore a still greater resemblance to the case here brought forward by his Lordship; the extent and condition of their tenure varied from those of a jagheerdar, or feudal chieftain, to those of a Government agent for the collection of the rents, invested with authority over the ryots, to enforce the cultivation of the lands, and to yield them, at the same time, his protection. In all cases, and under whatever designation, the collection of the revenue, and the appropriation of a part of it for defraying the local expenses, was the principal stipulation; and the amount which remained after these payments, over and above the remuneration allowed by the state, was paid into the treasury, either in the form of an offering, or present, on renewal of the jagheerdar's commission every three years, or of tribute, or simply in the form of land revenue. If this view had been adopted by the Indian Government at the time of making the permanent settlement, and if the zemindars had been compelled to grant pottahs to all the farmers or under tenants, and ryots, who could command sufficient capital to enable them to keep their lands in cultivation, the otherwise insurmountable difficulties arising out of a vain endeavour to reconcile the existence of proprietary rights, with a denial of that control which a landholder everywhere possesses over his tenants, would have been in the first instance avoided; and the zemindar would have fallen into his natural and correct position, of assistant to the collector of the district, in remitting through him the net land revenue to Government, after paying the authorised local expenses.

In addition, however, to the various arguments by which the question of the permanent settlement, and the persons with whom that settlement was to be made, had, not undesignedly, been perplexed, two other considerations were not without their influence upon the minds of the Court of Directors and the principal members of the Indian Government. The first was the actual necessity for realizing quickly and certainly the greatest possible revenue from India, in consequence of the commercial embarrassments into which the Company had fallen; and the Court of Directors were only too happy to close with a plan which yielded even more than they had calculated upon, without feeling disposed to attend to the developement of any other system, the operation of which might not turn out so speedily advantageous to their interests. The other, a consideration which may be supposed to have had much weight with the Indian Government, and to have induced them to recognise the zemindars as proprietors of the soil, in preference to the ryots, was, that the Government itself stood in the position of a zemindar in respect to its salt as well as to its opium monopolies; and whilst in this capacity it reserved to itself the right to alter the tenure of the ryot in the Salt Mehals, &c. it could not with any consistency consider the proprietary right to be vested in any but the zemindars.

Notwithstanding, therefore, the concurrence of all parties in the necessity for protecting the ryots, the latter were placed in subordination to the zemindars, with no other stipulation in their favour, in the act of permanent settlement, than an article,* declaring that it was "a duty at all times indispensably required from the proprietors of land to conduct themselves with good faith and moderation towards their dependant talookdars and ryots, and that Government reserved to itself the power to enact, whenever deemed proper to do so, such regulations as might be thought necessary for the protection and welfare of the dependant talookdars, ryots, and other cultivators of the soil." Regulations to this effect were indeed subsequently framed, and there is little doubt that if the same coolness of judgment and strict impartiality which had so much influence in enacting the

* Colebrook's Supplement, p. 358.

permanent settlement, had superintended* its operations for two or three years, it would, in spite of the disadvantages under which it laboured, have answered every reasonable expectation; but the departure of Lord Cornwallis to Europe so soon after the great change had been effected, left the new system in the hands of some of its bitterest enemies, and the want of cordial co-operation on the part of the civil functionaries, by which the measure had all along been impeded, quickly ensured its virtual abrogation. Accord-

* Mr. Tucker, however, seems to be of a different opinion. Not only does he think that the several Governors of India were peculiarly suited to the particular times and circumstances in which they happen to have been placed, but in the ardour of his optimism he asserts that Lord Teignmouth followed in the footsteps of his illustrious predecessor, and with scrupulous good faith gave effect to plans which, as a member of Lord Cornwallis's Government, he had felt it his duty to oppose. This is the first time, perhaps, that the individual by whom a plan was to be carried into effect, has been thought peculiarly suited to that task by his personal hostility to the measure. Whatever may have been the good faith of Lord Teignmouth, whether to his own or to his predecessor's opinion, certain it is, that the regulation which drove the ryots into the civil courts to ascertain their rate of lease, destroyed the very corner-stone of that fabric which Lord Cornwallis had been so intent upon rearing.—Tucker's Review, &c. p. 216.—See also Fifth Report, p. 486-7.

ingly, we find that a regulation (8 of 1763), which directed that landholders should prepare forms of pottahs, or leases, for the collector's approbation, and tender such pottahs to their tenants, on pain of being fined if they neglected to do so, was suspended in the following year in a great number of zillahs, and it was then declared that the approbation of the collector extended only to the form * of pottahs, " any dispute regarding the rate being referred to the civil courts." Here, then, we have at once the true cause of the vast accumulation of law-suits in the several courts: the pottahs, which the ryots had been taught to expect, were so much waste-paper, until their terms had been settled by an appeal to law; and as it is probable that it did not happen in abové one instance in ten that both parties agreed upon the subject, almost the whole agricultural population were actually compelled to appeal to the courts. Mr. Mill, in his History of British India, attributes the accumulation of undecided cases in a great measure to the mischievous prejudices of lawyers, " one of the most remarkable of which is that of rendering judicial proceedings intricate by the multiplication of technical forms,† &c. ;" and cer-

* Regulations 2 and 4, of 1794.

† History of British India, p. 283. *et seq.*

tainly the description of the forms and delays, including repeated translations of law-papers, given by Mr. Shore in his first minute * (already referred to), is sufficiently formidable. The 5th Report, indeed, expressly informs us, that the judicial rules upon which those still in use in Bengal are founded, "had the advantage of being framed by professional talents;" but this the historian seems to think is *per se* anything but a recommendation. The habits, ideas, and associations of professional men, are so inseparably connected with precedent and authority, that they are seldom well qualified for striking out new paths in legislation: blinded, like horses in a mill, they are apt to imagine that they are making great strides in advance, when they have only been travelling in the old beaten track of the little circle to which they have so long been yoked. On this subject, however, the historian appears to be somewhat at variance with himself; for he informs us that "there was in India nothing which in reality deserved the name of law," forgetting what he had just said of the perverse ingenuity of lawyers, and that he had shortly before told his readers, that "justice had always been distributed in the method of simple and rational enquiry" among the people of Hin-

* Fifth Report, Appendix, p. 190.

dostan. We have the authority of the 5th Report for the fact of the people of India having been governed by a system in which they apparently acquiesced with cheerfulness, and that the customs of the Hindoo and Mohammedan law were known, if not to all the European Judges and Magistrates, certainly to the native law and ministerial officers, whose services, we are told, were common to all the English courts, district as well as city: the Mohammedan laws with respect to Mussulmen, and the Hindoo with respect to Hindoos, being considered the general rules by which the Judges were to form their decisions in all civil suits, and the Mohammedan law of the Koran, as explained by the commentators, the general rule for criminal justice; with such alterations and modifications of its sanguinary punishments and mutilations, as the milder spirit of British criminal justice dictated. With regard, however, to the principles on which English practice was engrafted upon Indian law, and particularly to the introduction of paid advocates * (vakeels), it

* Lord Cornwallis is not responsible for the introduction of vakeels into Indian Courts of Justice, as might be inferred from the passage of Mr. Mill's history here adverted to; his Lordship found them already established there by the regulations of 1781, and all he did was to reform the abuses connected with their practice and appointments.

is impossible not to agree with the historian in his general view of the law, not indeed in India only, but even in the mother country.

The absurdities by which English law still continues to be encumbered, arose in the course of ages out of peculiar states of society, and are retained apparently from no other motive than the instinctive horror of innovation, which the timid of all persuasions are too prone to entertain. The structure of society has undergone many and great changes, but the common law is still "in the rearward of the fashion," and retains its antiquated costume, as if unconscious of the ridicule with which it is covered. It evinces, however, a constant endeavour to reconcile new feelings and new circumstances to its own preconceived notions; and thus, by a sparing adoption of such modern improvements as bear a strained resemblance to ancient practice, it has become a thing of threads and patches,* utterly incomprehensible to ordinary men. Authority and precedent are its avowed foundation; and its professed aim is to furnish a plain and certain rule for the guidance and protection of all. Yet new decisions of indi-

* Questi sono, (says Beccaria,) gli espedienti delle nazioni deboli, le leggi delle quali non sono che istantanee riparazioni di un edificio ruinoso, che crolla da ogni parte.

vidual Judges, grounded upon fanciful analogies to some former case, are constantly erected into maxims of law, and an adherence to remote sources of authority, in opposition to the plain standard of reason and common sense, involves every fresh question in inextricable confusion. Thus, whilst the stability of the law is relied upon in theory, its uncertainty is notorious and apparently inevitable in practice; and decisions, in fact, depend more upon the personal character of the judge, than upon any fixed or ascertained principles. Under the hollow pretence, indeed, of shielding us from the tyranny or corruption of judges, by referring every thing to precedent, it, in reality, creates the worst of tyrannies,—a varying and uncertain law; and it sets, as it were, a premium upon the ingenuity of lawyers, to reconcile present circumstances with past decisions. Thus it furnishes a constant bar to its own improvement, by discarding every thing that has not some previous sanction in its favour, without adverting to the circumscribed state of knowledge and experience at the period when that sanction was pronounced; and it has a tendency to encourage litigation by holding out almost as fair a prospect of success to the wicked as to the innocent. What is termed common law, is, in fact, to be found only in reports of cases and in the *dicta* of judges, forming together an immense heterogeneous mass, which, on the one hand, may be made to assume any form by means of what is technically called a fiction, and from which, on the other, the ingenuity of a practised lawyer can extract authority for almost any doctrine however absurd. Right and wrong, in short, become in a great measure subordinate considerations; the sole question is, not what is just, but what is law; and that law is to be found not in any written enactment, but in the ever-varying opinion of presiding judges.

To fix this wavering mass, to give firmness and consistency to the loose elements of the soil, is indeed a great desideratum, not only in India, but in England also. All writers are agreed, that since the adoption of the Code Napoleon, the number of lawsuits for real property (precisely that department in which English law displays the greatest number of subtilties) has been greatly reduced in France. Indeed, the mere compression of existing laws into a small compass, is of itself a benefit conferred upon the community; it not only brings the law within the comprehension of all, but it confines the subject-matter of future comment, and restrains the authority of the judge within its just bounds—those of a faithful interpretation of the laws. For the framing and institution of such a code in India, an excellent opportunity was undoubtedly lost when the reforms of 1793 were carried into effect. The submissive character of the Hindoos, their acknowledged hereditary prostration, and their habits of looking up to their rulers as to their father, and, under Providence, their God upon earth,—were no less favourable to the calm and dispassionate investigation which such a measure would have demanded, than to the superintendence of its operation in the hands of the most considerate and well-informed servants of the Company. We are told, indeed, that it was necessary to respect the prejudices of the natives, and to adhere as much as possible to their laws and customs, in framing a system of Government for our eastern possessions; but a very slight inspection of the regulations, which have been passed under this solemn injunction, will convince any man, that the only prejudices which have been respected, are certain cruel and disgusting observances of their religion; which, in their operation, are rather calculated to assist,* than to impede

* See, amongst other instances, regulation 4, of 1806, for the care with which the most cruel and abominable superstitions practised at the Temple of Juggernaut have been sanctioned and organized with a view to the pecuniary profit which they yield to our Christian Government. The number of lives annually supposed to be sacrificed in consequence of the Juggernaut pilgrimage, is too great to mention; the surrounding country is literally whitened with human bones.

the fiscal views of Government; and that, in other respects, very little attention has been paid to the feelings or opinions of the people. We found the inhabitants of India, it is true, immersed in the most profound ignorance, and a prey to the most absurd and revolting superstition; but security of property, and redress of grievances, are substantial benefits, which address themselves to the business and bosoms of men of every intellect, and of all persuasions; and certainly, the conduct of the people of Bengal, in appealing to our law courts, did not evince any slowness to avail themselves of the protection which was offered to them, even by the very incomplete reforms effected at the period now referred to. This conduct, as the Government justly observes, indicated a change of circumstances which ought to be received with satisfaction, inasmuch as it evinced the protection intended to be afforded by an equal administration of justice, to be real and efficient; and showed that the care and attention, which its directors with so much solicitude had urged the Government to observe for preventing the oppressions formerly practised by the most powerful land-holders, had not been exerted in vain; and that in the success of those exertions a foundation had been laid for the happiness of the great body of the people, and in the increase of population, agriculture, and commerce, for the general prosperity of the country.* But the Government, with singular inconsistency, instead of acknowledging the confidence thus shown in the uprightness of their intentions by redoubling their efforts to administer strict and impartial justice to all parties, first did all in their power to promote litigation, and then loaded the redress of grievances with such heavy duties, as amounted to a denial of it altogether to the great majority of suitors. If the liberal and enlightened observation just cited, had been followed up by an increase in the number of courts, or by the appointment of commissioners, with power to settle all disputes arising out of the new order of things, upon the known and recognized principles of equity to the parties, it cannot be doubted that the rage for litigation would quickly have subsided, and that the permanent settlement would have realized the most favourable expectations, without that revolution in property, and those appalling scenes of distress, with which its operation has been accompanied. On the contrary, however, in less than a month after passing a regulation for the relief of the zemindars, another was published for re-enacting the payment of the institution fee, abolished in 1793, and for establishing fees on exhibits, " so as to render the proceed-

* Revenue Letter 31st October, 1799.

ings costly to the party cast or non-suited, without (it is said) discouraging recourse to them where the cause of action might be well founded." The preamble states that "in consequence of there being no expense in the first instance, and but a moderate and limited one ultimately, many groundless and litigious suits and complaints have been instituted against individuals, and the trials of others have been protracted, &c., whereby the judges have been prevented from determining causes with that expedition which is essential for deterring individuals from instituting vexatious claims, or refusing to satisfy just demands, &c.; and that the establishing of fees on the institution and trial of suits, and on petitions presented to the court, being considered to be the best mode of putting a stop to this abuse of the ready means now afforded to individuals of availing themselves of the exercise of the laws, without obstructing the bringing forward of just claims; the following rules are enacted, &c." The imposition of this expense, it is stated in the 5th Report, was expected to repress litigation in future; but with respect to the large accumulation of causes already on the judge's file, they were got rid of by an *ex-post facto* law, which directed that the fees required to be paid on the institution of suits hereafter (10th April 1795) "shall be paid, under the like rules and exceptions, in all suits or appeals now depending in the zillah, or city courts, &c. &c. which may have been instituted subsequent to the 1st May 1793, unless adjusted by the parties; and such suits, unless withdrawn, or the fees are paid within one month, to be dismissed." In thus endeavouring to repress litigation, however, most of the fees were carried to the account of Government, and their amount, no doubt, suggested the expediency of turning what was now considered a national characteristic, to the advantage of the state, by farther impositions; accordingly a regulation to this effect was passed in 1797. But in thus converting the views of their subjects into a species of traffic, the Indian Government seems to have been aware that some apology was due; and on that account the abolition of the police tax is made in some measure the excuse for increasing the fees on the institution and trials of suits, and for establishing a stamp duty on law papers. "Difficulties, (it is said in the preamble to the regulation in question, 6th of 1797) having been experienced in determining what persons were liable to be charged with the police tax, and frauds and exactions having in consequence been committed by the assessors and collectors, to the vexation of the contributors as well as to the diminution of the produce of the tax, the Vice-President in Council has *therefore* resolved to abolish this tax; and with a view farther to discourage the preferring of litigious complaints, and the filing of superfluous exhibits, and the summoning unnecessary witnesses on the trial of suits, and also to provide for the deficiency which will be occasioned in the public revenue by the abolition of the police tax, as well as to add to the public resources without burthening individuals, he has resolved," &c. &c. Passing over the singular manner in which the discouragement of litigious complaints is joined with the abolition of a totally distinct tax, acknowledged to be nearly unproductive, it may be observed that as the fees and stamps were here made payable alike by those who might prefer just complaints, as by those who might be termed litigious, it is difficult to understand how such a tax could be considered as not burthening individuals. On the contrary, no tax burthens individuals so much as a tax upon law proceedings, to which no person resorts but in asserting or defending a right, of which he is, or is threatened to be, unjustly deprived. A police tax, on the contrary, being nothing more than a general contribution for a common benefit, is, under equitable regulations, an imposition every way unobjectionable, and by municipal arrangements might certainly be collected and disbursed, not only to the advantage of the state, but to the great comfort and security of the public.

The difficulty of keeping pace with the demands for redress, does not appear to have been sensibly diminished by the abovementioned regulations: on the contrary, their tendency being to encourage injustice by hopes of impunity, the natural consequences ought to have been rather an increase than a diminution of suits at law; but it was not till the year 1803, that the proper remedy was applied, by adding to the number of judges throughout the provinces, and enlarging the jurisdiction of the native commissioners or munsiffs. This remedy, however, was applied on so small a scale as to be totally inadequate to the end proposed; and the usual consolation for such a failure was again sought in an augmentation of the revenue, by means of farther stamp duties. Accordingly, Regulation 1st of 1814, and others which followed after a short interval, increase the rate of stamp duties, and extend the use of stamp paper so greatly, that without them no complaint can be filed, no grievance taken cognizance of;*

* Harrington's Analysis, vol. i. p. 162, apparently cites this regulation as first introducing the use of stamps "for raising a revenue;" but the preamble above quoted from Regulation 6th, 1797, shows the principle to have been avowed on that occasion.

on the contrary, if any suitor neglect to provide himself with the necessary stamps, and present documents written on common paper, he is sentenced to a fine of twenty times the value of the stamp omitted, and a rejection of his complaint until the fine be paid and the prescribed stamps supplied.

Meantime, however, the power of distraint had been greatly increased by Regulation 7th of 1799, by which it was declared that under-tenants of every description were to be considered defaulters for any arrears of rent withheld beyond the day on which the same might have been payable; and liable to immediate distress, if all such arrears were not paid on demand. A commission of one anna in the rupee on the amount of sales of property sold was also authorized to be charged to the account of the defaulters, in addition to the other expenses attending the attachment. The power of the collector was also strengthened by his being allowed to imprison defaulting land-holders, and to charge interest for the amount of the monthly instalment remaining undischarged, at the rate of one per cent. *per mensem*, from the date at which the arrear became due, without waiting for authority from the Board of Revenue so to do, unless he think proper to apply for special instructions. He was authorized and directed, however, to suspend the exercise of these powers in cases of drought, inundation, or other calamity of the season, and where the defaulter was entirely blameless, reporting circumstances to the Board of Revenue. But whether from the Board having condemned this indulgence where shown, or from the natural inclination of men in official stations to exceed the bounds of their authority, the collectors did, notwithstanding, attach and distrain to such an extent as to call for the interference of Government * to prohibit their doing so, during the three first months of the year, whilst the landholders and farmers were adjusting their settlements with the ryots. By the regulation here referred to, however, it was directed that, in order to limit the division of property, when an estate was attached, the whole of it, and not a part, was to be sold; the surplus produce of such sale, after discharging the amount of arrears, interest, and fines, to be given to the proprietor, *unless otherwise specially directed.* It was moreover ordained, that whenever the collector *thought* the revenue was wilfully withheld, or the arrear ascribable to neglect, mismanagement, or misconduct, the *Board* might impose an additional penalty of one per cent. *per mensem,* to be paid from the time when the arrears became due till dis-

* Reg. 1. of 1801.

charged, or till the farm or estate was attached, together with distress and sale of personal property where accounts were not forthcoming. If, however, the proprietor at any time antecedent to the sale, delivers in his account, the sale is not to take place; but instead thereof, as a punishment to the defaulter for his withholding his accounts, the Governor General may impose such fines as he may judge proper, in *addition* to the former.

Here then may be said to have terminated the long struggle between the zemindars and the ryots on the one hand, and the Government and the zemindars on the other. At first the zemindars were relieved from the liability to imprisonment, and other arbitrary punishments for non-payment of their revenue; but portions of their estates were ordered to be sold to make good their defalcations; when, however, they complained of this, the power of imprisonment was restored, and their personal property, as well as their whole estates, rendered liable to sale. In like manner, the ryots were apparently secured in the possession of their ground, by the zemindars being directed to grant them pottahs or leases, and they were encouraged to appeal to the law when oppressed by their landlord:—their availing themselves of this privilege, however, occasioned the imposition of law taxes, the restoration of the power of distraint and imprisonment, formerly held over them by the zemindars, and eventually the establishment of stamp duties, to such extent and amount as almost to constitute a total denial of redress under any grievances they might suffer.

There can be no doubt, however, that the permanent settlement, though ruinous to the greater part of the old zemindars, has greatly contributed to extend cultivation; and that the present zemindars, as a body, and indeed with exception of those whose waste land estates are now in fact under sequestration, are in a very prosperous condition. This circumstance, indeed, is so well known that, as before remarked, it has excited what was termed by Mr. Shore, "the cupidity of Government," to demand a portion of the excess. It must not, however, be supposed, because some individuals have prospered greatly under the new order of things, that, therefore, the land tax is moderate; for as yet the scanty and penurious husbandry of the country has experienced no general improvement. The advantages referred to have been mostly confined to those estates which contained a large portion of uncultivated land, or the boundaries of which had been but loosely ascertained, or in which the cultivation had been improved by the unexpected demand for more valuable produce. In all these instances it is probable that a rise of rents was accomplished without much difficulty; but the number of cases in point, in which any great degree of improvement was attended with an augmentation of the zemindars' income, must have borne but an inconsiderable proportion to the general mass. It may be observed, too, that in addition to the slowness and uncertainty of returns from the cultivation of waste lands in general, the appropriation of pasture land is attended with a diminution of apparent profit, by the increased expense and difficulty of subsisting the cattle used for agricultural purposes, particularly during that period of the year when the crop is on the ground. But even were the fact otherwise, were it certain that every zemindar had doubled his income by the improvements effected on his estate, how unworthy it is of the character of a great Government to endeavour, by every means in its power, to deprive its subjects of their hard-earned profits, because after so many years of risk and labour those profits turn out to be greater than could have been expected, under so severe an assessment. How much more wise, as well as humane, it would be to rejoice in the unexpected prosperity of the country, to encourage accumulation, and with it, increased activity of trade, and a sincere attachment to the Government which secured to them the enjoyment of so many blessings! Instead of this, however, the natives are continually alarmed by inquisitions, actual or threatened, into the validity of their titles, and correct measurement of their estates; and swarms of canongoes, or native revenue surveyors, are spread over the surface of the country, ostensibly for the protection of the ryots, but in reality for the purpose of discovering and reporting unassessed land. These men, who are virtually released from responsibility, partly by their own obscurity, but chiefly by the small number and inaccessibility of the English functionaries under whom they act, extort money almost at will from the individuals with whose lands they have any concerns, and by indulgences to one, or menaces to another, afflict the unhappy people with endless vexations.

In order more clearly to point out the condition of the ryots, the following table of the produce of one biggah, about $\frac{1}{3}$ of an English acre, together with the usual rent according to the annual settlement, and expenses of cultivation, is here inserted. A comparison with the estimate given by Colebrooke, (Husbandry of Bengal,) will show that, whatever may be the case with other classes, the situation of the ryot has not improved. All the articles here inserted, with the exception, perhaps, of paddy, are susceptible of great increase; and some garden-lands, particularly in the vicinity of large towns, produce five and even ten times as much; but taking a large extent of country, the average is not greater than what is here given: this point, however, is not of such importance regarding the whole calculation, from the small proportion of land appropriated to the sort of produce in question, one tenth of the whole cultivated surface being considered much more than its utmost extent.

| Description of Produce. | Expense of Seed, Cultivation, Reaping, Weeding, and Storing. | | Rent. | | Total. | | Value of the Crop. | Cultivator's Surplus. | |
|---|---|---|---|---|---|---|---|---|---|
| | Rps. | Ans. | Rps. | Ans. | Rps. | Ans. | Rps. | Rps. | Ans. |
| Paddy { Old Land | 3 | 1 | 1 | 8 | 4 | 9 | 8 | 3 | 7 |
| Paddy { New Land | 3 | 0 | 0 | 12 | 3 | 12 | 7 | 3 | 4 |
| Sugar Cane | 10 | 4 | 5 | 0 | 15 | 4 | 20 | 4 | 12 |
| Tobacco | 9 | 12 | 5 | 0 | 14 | 12 | 20 | 5 | 4 |
| Ginger | 9 | 4 | 5 | 0 | 14 | 4 | 20 | 5 | 12 |
| Cotton | 6 | 4 | 5 | 0 | 11 | 4 | 18 | 6 | 12 |
| Onions | 10 | 4 | 5 | 0 | 15 | 4 | 22 | 6 | 12 |
| Potatoes | 6 | 12 | 5 | 0 | 11 | 12 | 16 | 4 | 4 |
| Garlic | 10 | 4 | 5 | 0 | 15 | 4 | 20 | 4 | 12 |
| Curry, Herbs, &c. | 6 | 12 | 4 | 0 | 10 | 12 | 16 | 5 | 4 |
| Jute | 4 | 12 | 2 | 8 | 7 | 4 | 11 | 3 | 12 |
| Hemp | 4 | 12 | 4 | 0 | 8 | 12 | 14 | 5 | 4 |
| Turmeric | 7 | 12 | 4 | 0 | 11 | 12 | 17 | 5 | 4 |
| Mustard | 4 | 12 | 3 | 0 | 7 | 12 | 12 | 4 | 4 |
| Mulberry | 5 | 12 | 2 | 8 | 8 | 4 | 12 | 3 | 12 |
| Pulse, of sorts | 5 | 4 | 2 | 8 | 7 | 12 | 11 | 3 | 4 |
| Wheat | 5 | 12 | 2 | 8 | 8 | 4 | 13 | 4 | 12 |
| Barley | 5 | 8 | 2 | 8 | 8 | 0 | 12 | 4 | 0 |
| Cucumbers | 9 | 12 | 5 | 0 | 14 | 12 | 21 | 6 | 4 |

If, then, we suppose a farm to consist of about 25 biggahs, or 8⅓ English acres, which is as much as one man and his family can manage, the cultivator's surplus, at the above average, will be about $12\frac{1}{2}$ rupees for the garden land, and $74\frac{1}{2}$ for the rice land, making altogether 87 rupees, or 8*l.* 7*s.* per annum, or 7 rupees 4 annas for the monthly subsistence of himself and family.

The following is a statement of the expense of living for a family of five persons, on the lowest scale consistent with bare subsistence:

| | Rup. | Ans. |
|---|---|---|
| Rice four-fifths of a seer, about $1\frac{3}{4}$lbs. for each person, at 30 seers per rupee - - | 4 | 0 |
| Pulse, one pice, (less than a halfpenny) per diem each - - - - - - | 2 | $5\frac{1}{2}$ |
| Salt and Condiments ditto (salt at 5 maunds per rupee - - - - - - | 1 | $2\frac{3}{4}$ |
| Oil, two chittacks (about 2oz.) at 10 rupees per maund - - - - - - | 0 | 15 |
| Total | 8 | $7\frac{1}{4}$ |

To this must be added something for clothing, scanty as it is, besides occasional expenses for repairs of hut, fees, &c. Charity should also enter into the account, but as this is generally bestowed in the form of victuals, it is difficult to estimate its exact value; as, however, it actually diminishes the above allowance, and that in no inconsiderable degree, it should not be lost sight of in forming an opinion of the condition of the people. The item of charity, indeed, is much larger than can readily be conceived by those who are unacquainted with the habits of an Indian community. The class of people living entirely upon alms, whether given from motives of superstition, or from mere compassion, is exceedingly great. Crowds of sturdy beggars, generally of a religious caste, parade the country, and extort a plentiful subsistence, more from the united effect of fear and superstition, than from any other feeling of the inhabitants. Every village, also, has its separate band of religious mendicants, who make their rounds every day, demanding a handful of rice from each householder; and if to these we add the really destitute objects, who from disease or infirmity have a claim upon the compassion of their more fortunate brethren, we shall have a mass of charitable demands, from which the almost unhoused Hindoo has no refuge but by granting a portion of his scanty meal, almost equal to the poor's rate in England, burthensome as that is acknowledged to be.

The only methods which the poor husbandman has of eking out his miserable existence, are by disposing of the produce of such fruit trees as may be upon his farm, or by keeping cows and selling their produce; or lastly, by endeavouring to raise a second crop of some kind in the intervals of the usual harvests. But from all these sources of profit so much must be deducted for interest of money, or encroachment upon other branches of his industry, that little or no benefit can be expected from them, in the present state of the country. Thus the produce of trees may be valuable in many cases, but they are prejudicial to the growth of other articles, and the ground they cover forms a serious deduction from the quantity of land cultivated: some indeed are attended with loss, unless more care is taken to strengthen the soil, than a poor ryot can afford; of this kind are plaintains, which, in addition to the usual fallow of one-fourth, or even one-third of the lands yearly, exhaust the soil in three or four years, and render it useless for a period much more than equal to the advantage to be derived from their culture. In like manner the profits of the dairy are realized at the expense of that share of the produce consumed by the cattle, together with the additional trouble, whatever it may be, of watching and milking them. In circumstances so straitened, even the smallest item becomes of importance, and the miserable hut in which the cultivator resides must be considered as diminishing, *pro tanto*, the quantity of his productive land.

If by the above table we endeavour to ascertain the present situation of the zemindars, the following will be the calculation, assuming that the increase of rent since the permanent settlement has not much exceeded the proportionate increase in the cultivation of the more valuable articles of produce, which is generally supposed to be the fact. The zemindar's share of the rent of the 25 biggahs, above mentioned, would be only 6 rupees 5 annas per annum; but supposing him to possess 1000 biggahs or about 354 acres, his income would be 252½ rupees, and the amount of land revenue paid by him to Government 2272½ rupees. But to his income must be added the profit arising from any uncultivated or unassessed land, which happened to be upon his estate at the period of the settlement, and from which he has since been able to raise a rent by bringing it under tillage. The quantity of land exempted from taxation (rent free), and that which was appropriated to pasturage taken together, was calculated by Mr. J. Grant* at no less than two-fifths of the whole surface in 1786, whilst the land in cultivation was but one-half that amount or one-fifth of the whole; and as Colebrooke (Husbandry &c.) apparently estimates the rent of free lands as in the proportion of 3 to 4 to the waste land, we have upon these data the average quantity of reclaimable land in each estate equal to something more than one-third of the whole. But as it was clearly the interest of the land-

* See the Analysis already referred to, in the Appendix, 5th Report.

holder to cultivate as much of his ground as possible during the several settlements which were made immediately previous to, and which formed the basis of, the permanent settlement in 1793, (since he paid rent for the whole,) it is reasonable to suppose that a considerable portion of it was rendered productive during the seven years which elapsed between the periods referred to. Allowing, however, that this may not have been the fact, and calculating upon every spot of ground, even to the total absorption of pasturage, having been cultivated by the present proprietors, it will only amount to about 340 biggahs in 1000; which, upon the average rent given in the foregoing table, will make 858½ rupees; which, added to the former 252, will amount to 1110½ rupees (111*l.* per annum), or 92½ per mensem; a very small income, indeed, for the support of a zemindar and his family, and the payment of the expenses necessarily attendant upon his rank and station.

But, besides that the above calculation is obviously an extreme and improbable one, it is generally believed that a very great majority of the present landholders pay no more than 500 rupees yearly to Government,—they consequently have only 55½ rupees for their income, out of the rents collected upon the assessment; and if to this we add * half the amount, as a reasonable average for tax-free cultivation, their miserable pittance is not more than that of the poorest class of ryots. Upon the whole, then, we may conclude that, with the utmost possible advantage that can be obtained under the present circumstances of the country, the great majority of landholders, as well as ryots, can realize nothing more than a bare subsistence from their ground; and that, from the impoverished state of the cultivating classes in general, there is no probability that their unassisted exertions will enable them to accumulate capital for the improvement of their stock, or for the encouragement of new branches of industry.

Hitherto, the poverty of the cultivating classes, men who have both property and employment, has alone been adverted to; but the extreme misery to which the immense mass of the unemployed population are reduced, would defy the most able pen adequately to describe, or the most fertile imagination to conceive. The extremes to which they are driven for subsistence may be judged of from the following facts, which, it is to be presumed, are well known to those who have resided for

* According to Colebrooke, their incomes are tripled, and in some instances they are said to have been decupled; but both cases must be exceedingly rare, the consequence of some extraordinary local circumstance.

any long period in India; but the number of helpless wretches who daily sink under the effects of misery and starvation, no attempt can be made to estimate.

On many occasions of ceremony in the families of wealthy individuals, it is customary to distribute alms to the poor; sometimes four annas, (about three pence,) and rarely more than eight annas each. When such an occurrence is made known, the poor assemble in astonishing numbers, and the roads are covered with them from twenty to fifty miles in every direction. On their approaching the place of gift, no notice is taken of them, though half famished and almost unable to stand, till towards the evening; when they are called into an enclosed space, and huddled together for the night in such crowds, that, notwithstanding their being in the open air, it is surprising how they escape suffocation. When the individual, who makes the donation, perceives that all the applicants are in the enclosure, (by which process he guards against the possibility of any poor wretch receiving his bounty twice,) he begins to dispense his alms, either in the night or on the following morning, by taking the poor people, one by one, from the place of their confinement, and driving them off as soon as they have received their pittance. The number of people thus accumulated generally amounts to from twenty to fifty thousand; and from the distance they travel, and the hardships they endure for so inconsiderable a bounty, some idea may be formed of their destitute condition.

In the interior of Bengal, there is a class of inhabitants who live by catching fish in the ditches and rivulets; the men employing themselves during the whole day, and the women travelling to the nearest city, often a distance of 15 miles, to sell the produce. The rate at which these poor creatures perform their daily journey is almost incredible, and the sum realized is so small as scarcely to afford them the necessaries of life.* In short, throughout the whole provinces, the crowds of poor wretches who are destitute of the means of subsistence are beyond belief: on passing through the country, they are seen to pick the undigested grains of food from the dung of elephants, horses, and camels; and if they can procure a little salt, large parties of them sally into the fields at night, and devour the green blades of corn or rice, the instant they are seen to shoot

* This source of profit, insignificant as it is, together with that arising from ferries, did not escape the searching eye of Government; and Regulation 19. of 1816, and 6. of 1819, ordained taxes upon each: these taxes, however, it has since been found expedient to repeal, as unproductive.

above the surface; such, indeed, is their wretchedness, that they envy the lot of the convicts working in chains upon the roads, and have been known to incur the danger of a criminal prosecution, in order to secure themselves from starving by the allowance made to those who are condemned to hard labour.

# CHAPTER IV.

## ON THE GENERAL CHARACTER AND TEMPER OF THE NATIVES OF BRITISH INDIA.

"Dum alii quoquo modo audita pro compertis habent, alii vera in contrarium vertunt, et gliscit utrumque posteritate."

It is a favourite maxim with a large class of politicians, and particularly with those connected with India, that what the sword has conquered, the sword must maintain. If this maxim be intended to keep up the vigilance of the conqueror, until the conquered become reconciled to their change of condition, it is hardly necessary to inculcate it with the oracular solemnity which some writers have done; since a conquest can only be said to be complete when opposition has entirely ceased, and the minds of the vanquished have been restored to their wonted tranquillity. But if, as seems to be the aim of some late writers on the affairs of India, it be meant that a nation which has been conquered by the sword, must ever be retained in its allegiance by the same means, the maxim is equally false and pernicious.

It assumes the people to be constantly in a state of revolt; it rejects all sympathy with them; and tacitly admitting that one foreign government, however long established, can be entitled to no preference over any other that may endeavour to supplant it, leaves the nation in dispute to be fought for, like the prey of wild beasts, with the sole privilege of being devoured by the victor.

The first object of a conqueror ought to be to conciliate the conquered, and to discover materials for his and their joint security against foreign aggression. He should reflect, that the same prowess which put him in possession, may suffice to expel him, if superior means of repelling an attack be not brought into motion. The very facility with which he made the acquisition becomes a principal cause of his insecurity; for, whilst the value of the conquest continues to offer the same temptation, the means by which he achieved it are known to the world, and are capable of being accurately estimated in the event of attack; so that he is liable at any time to be assailed by superior forces when the spirit of the community over which he rules is not taken into the account; and that spirit is a reserve of strength, or a source of danger, according as he succeeds in exciting their confidence, and uniting their interest with his own.

The greater part of our Indian territory has now been under British sway for nearly a century, and our conquest may still, in the language of Burke, be said to be as crude as it was the first day: we govern without society and without sympathy of the natives; we have no more social habits with the people than if we still resided in England; nor, indeed, any species of intercourse with them, but that which is necessary to making a sudden fortune with a view to a remote settlement;—yet at the present day, when so little has been done by us for India, orators in Leadenhall Street still speak of our being too prone to innovation, and of our being misled by our habits of judging the people by the scale of civilization to which we ourselves have advanced. We are too apt, it is said, to overlook the state of comparative non-civilization to which the now enlightened English nation was itself reduced, during that eventful period of its history, when bigotry, superstition, and prejudice were its sad and sole characteristics, and to forget that our emancipation from the bonds of darkness was effected, not by any sudden or coercive reformation, but by the gradual hand of time, the unshackled reflections of reason, and the salutary influence of the great principles of truth, which have at length placed us in a permanent and intellectual superiority. But if there be any truth in this eulogium on our moral feeling and intellectual superiority, we have at least had ample time to impart a portion of the benefit of them to the natives of our Indian empire. There is no reason why those who travel upon the road to civilization and knowledge should be compelled to follow, step by step, in the track of those who first explored the way. To the latter, the route was necessarily long and wearisome, from their ignorance of the true direction, and the want of any guide to conduct their steps; but no sooner were they arrived at the summit of the ascent, than the commanding view which they obtained enabled them to detect the needless wanderings into which they had been seduced, and to point out a plainer way to all succeeding travellers, free from the difficulties and dangers by which the first adventurers had been embarrassed. This, however, it appears, is by no means the process to be followed in India; but the natives are to be left almost entirely to their unassisted energies, with little or no assistance from the superior knowledge and experience possessed by those who assume the office of their protectors.

There are men who seem to imagine that such of their fellow-creatures as have the misfortune to differ from them in complexion are, like horses and dogs, incapable of imparting to others any portion of the individual training bestowed upon them by their masters. "In speaking of the Hindoos," says Mr. Rickards, "something mysterious is always fancied to belong to them, as if they were not composed of flesh and blood, nor had passions and desires as the rest of the human species." Undoubtedly, if the present generation of civilized man were to rest content with continuing their race, and furnishing their children with nothing but food and raiment, Europe would in no very long period become as barbarous, not only as the rude parts of Hindostan, but as the most savage regions of Africa; but this at once we pronounce impossible, from the tendency, which is the peculiar characteristic of the human mind, to advance in wisdom and intelligence. Yet this impossibility we do our utmost to render not only possible, but almost inevitable, in Hindostan, by systematically denying to the natives in general all access to useful instruction, and repressing all attempts to improve them, by stigmatizing such conduct as dangerous to the stability of our political rule. The argument against the diffusion of knowledge among the lower classes, though it assumes in India the political type which is peculiar to that Government, is, in fact, the same throughout the world,—that education is unnecessary to those who, from their poverty, are destined to labour for their subsistence: as if the desire to improve our condition were not, under all circumstances, the stimulus to our exertions; and as if the degree of natural intelligence with which an individual was endowed, were not as susceptible of being improved to his advantage, as his manual dexterity or muscular strength. As, however, a great portion of the wealthy, from indolence as well as from jealousy, are more anxious to maintain their position by repressing the energies of others than by exerting their own, they are almost unanimous in the apprehensions they entertain of the fearful effect of that buoyancy which would be evinced, if genius and industry were, under all circumstances, assured of a fair field in the general competition for the good things of this life. Hence the sneers so assiduously thrown out against what is termed the march of intellect in Europe, and the rancour with which all extended endeavours to improve the moral condition of the subject millions of our Indian provinces, are met by those whose vested interests are, however erroneously, conceived to be endangered by such a measure. If an adherent of the Company be asked what objection there is to granting the Hindoos the benefit of education, with a view to their participating in those civil rights which are at present exclusively in the hands of Europeans, he replies, 'That they are not yet in a state to enable them to profit by such a boon;' and thus, the effect being taken for the cause, misgovernment is to be continued, because it has been found to produce injurious consequences. So in the queries circulated to the judicial authorities of Bombay in 1822, relatively to the establishment of trial by jury*, one Judge has so little reliance on the probity or independent spirit of the natives, that he thinks they would seldom, if ever, act in opposition to what they conceived to be the wish, or even opinion, of the judge. Another speaks of the acknowledged want of integrity in the native character, which, according to him, is so great, that natives will not place confidence in each other in punchayets, or arbitrations of a civil nature; or, if they do, they seldom fail to repent it: and others are decidedly against the plan, as foreign to the habits of the people, and inconsistent with their political situation. And thus it is, that by continually reasoning in a circle, the ignorance, wretchedness, and vice of the natives are ever destined to endure, because a hundred years of British protection and government have failed in producing any thing else.

Probably there is no region in the world in

* A regulation for trial by a jury of natives has, however, been passed by the Madras Government.

which the inhabitants are so entirely what their religion and civil government have made them, as the Hindoos. With some classes of Christians, auricular confession is supposed to be sufficient to keep the minds of men in subjection to a vigilant priesthood; and in China, a regulated system of precedence and individual authority secures the outward submission of all; but with the Hindoo, the constant interference of the injunctions of his religion in every action of his life, is calculated to repress both his mental and physical exertions, and to reduce him to the condition of a mere living machine. From this state of torpor he can only be awakened by being brought into collision with men of more active propensities, and of a higher order of intellect. To civilise him, we must first teach him to feel his wants, and to be sensible of his natural strength. A people like the Hindoos, might for ever, as they have already done for ages, continue to look upon themselves as a favoured race in the system of Providence, if not roused by the example of greater happiness and enjoyment in other states of existence: but it would be contrary to the character which human nature everywhere exhibits, to suppose that if the effect of useful knowledge, aided by moral and upright conduct, were fairly placed before them, they would fail to inspire a feeling of emulation, and an earnest desire for instruction; or that their absurd superstitions would not gradually wear away under such circumstances. Without this opportunity being afforded them, however, it is no less unfair to speculate upon their character, than to estimate the strength of a man whilst bound and loaded with chains.

Those who endeavour to open the eyes of the people of England, as to the true situation of their fellow-creatures in India, labour under considerable disadvantages from the immense extent of country, and the great variety of human character to which their speculations relate, no less than from the want of that intercourse with the natives which alone could enable them to form a correct estimate of their peculiar qualities. It falls to the lot of very few Europeans during their sojourn in India, to see any very considerable portion of the country subject to British rule; and of the few who have seen much, but a small number possess the talent to observe, or the inclination to record their observations. Most of those who are much engaged in the interior are men of business, who cannot, indeed, often command sufficient leisure to accumulate facts and inferences relating to any thing beyond the line of their own immediate occupation; whilst the comparatively idle men, who abound in the three great resorts of adventurers of all descriptions—Calcutta, Madras, and Bombay—are too apt to imagine that the specimens of the native population which they there meet with, are common to the whole of India. Yet, when we consider that the Bengal Presidency alone is nearly equal in size to France and Switzerland taken together, we shall cease to wonder that so few are competent to pronounce upon even that portion of our empire, still less that scarcely any remarks can apply, with equal accuracy, to the whole of the extensive regions of which it is composed. Of the public servants of the three Presidencies, probably those of Madras have the most general knowledge of the country in which they act. The fact, of the direction of all the great rivers of that part of India lying across the principal lines of communication from the capital to the interior, and consequently affording little or no convenience to travellers, is favourable to the incidental acquisition of topographical and statistical knowledge ; whereas the long and comparatively narrow tract of the Bengal presidency, being traversed from one extremity to the other by the noble rivers Ganges and Jumna, with their innumerable tributary streams, the principal communications are by water ; a mode of travelling of all others the least favourable for acquiring a knowledge of the country which is traversed. Such, indeed, are the conveniences afforded by this mode of conveyance, that travellers avoid even the smallest land journeys, and shutting themselves up in their accommodation-boats, which are frequently as large and commodious as private dwellings, they continue their customary occupations, without paying more attention to external objects than during an ordinary sea voyage. On this account, principally, the gentlemen who have resided in Bengal, independently of the great number who never quit Calcutta, are generally less acquainted with the state of the country, and the character of its inhabitants, from personal observation, than those of either of the other Presidencies.

Probably the most comprehensive description of Hindostan is to be met with in Sultan Baber's Memoirs. It is as follows:—" Hindostan is a country that has few pleasures to recommend it: the people are not handsome; they have no idea of the charms of friendly society, of frankly mixing together, or of familiar intercourse. They have no genius, no comprehension of mind, no politeness of manner, no kindness or fellow-feeling, no ingenuity or mechanical invention in planning or executing their handicraft works, no skill or knowledge in design or architecture; they have no good horses, no good flesh, no grapes or musk, melons,* no good fruits, no ice or cold water, no good food or bread in their bazars, no baths or colleges, no candles, no torches, not a candlestick!" In this spirited and faithful sketch, so characteristic of the habits of thought and observation of the distinguished writer, it is remarkable, that there is not a word either of the inferior personal strength of the Hindoos, their inhospitality† and

* Baber appears to have introduced grapes and melons into Hindostan, and from the following passage it might be inferred that the date was not unknown there. "They say that the date alone, of all the vegetable kingdom, resembles the animal kingdom in two respects: the one is, that where you cut off the head of an animal it perishes; and if you cut off the top of the date-tree it withers and dies: the other is, that as no animal bears without concourse with the male; in like manner, if you do not bring a branch of the male date-tree and shake it over the female, it bears no fruit." The introduction of the male date-tree into Hindostan (the female alone existing there at present), would be a great boon bestowed upon the inhabitants; no less, probably, than that of potatoes, for which they are understood to be indebted to their intercourse with Europe. The fructification of the date-tree, however, is a matter of some difficulty, where the male trees do exist. At the Isle of France, native Arabs are employed for that purpose.

† The rude state of the law at the period referred to, or it might perhaps be more correctly said, the non-existence of any laws, in the modern acceptation of the term, may be thought to account for the omission of litigiousness as one of the characteristics of a Hindoo; but there is reason to be-

litigiousness, or their want of courage,—topics upon which modern writers are so prone to expatiate.

"The muscular strength of the Hindoos," says Mr. Mill,* on the authority of various writers, "is small; even less, according to Mr. Orme, than the appearance of their bodies, though expressive of weakness, would lead the spectator to infer; and this is in some measure attributed to the simplicity and lightness of their food. But if this observation may be considered applicable to the Bengalese, and to the inhabitants of the Carnatic, what shall we say of the tribes under the government of the Polygars of the South, or of those in the interior of India, from the table-land of the Mysore to the provinces of Bundlecund and Rajpootanah; or to the inhabitants living on the banks of the Ganges, from its confluence with the Soane and Gogra, up to Hurdwar? countries in which the human form attains a degree of perfection, and strength, and stature, probably not surpassed by any people in Europe. The idea, in-

lieve that the *fureead kutcheree*, or public audience of justice, in which the sovereign and his subordinate governors were accessible to all, received all petitions, and enquired into them upon the spot, was in use long before the introduction of the law of the Koran in India.

* Hist. of India, p. 311.

deed, that vegetable food, accompanied by abstinence from fermented drink, prevents the increase of bodily strength, is a mere prejudice; and without enquiring by what subtle chemistry the nourishment we take is converted into blood and muscle, it is sufficient to advert to the condition of some of the larger quadrupeds, and to instance the elephant, the camel, the horse, and ox, in proof of the attainment of muscular strength, and a capacity for enduring fatigue, without the use of animal food. The observation of Forster on the robust activity of the people of Khorasan and Afghanistan, also quoted by Mr. Mill, in a note upon a passage in which the assumed corporeal weakness of the Hindoos is in some measure attributed to the climate, is, indeed, directly to this point; and a reference to the pages of Herodotus, where the discipline of the ancient Persians is described, would show that a light and simple diet was in olden time common in nations most celebrated for their strength and prowess. Nay more, at the present day, the condition of the Irish and Scotch, and many of the English peasantry, together with that of large masses of the population of the South of Europe, who seldom know what it is to obtain a meal of animal food, would afford farther proof, if required, to establish the same point.

With respect, too, to the litigiousness of the Hindoos, it may be observed, that the minute legislation which their system displays, by rendering almost every act of their life a religious obligation, puts it in the power of every individual to support himself by a reference to authority; and by enlisting his conscience on every occasion, gives an air of fanatical obstinacy to all their disputes. It is this circumstance that makes the Hindoo so tenacious of his rights in the first instance; whilst the general wretchedness of the people contributes to encourage that disposition; —men will ever cling with the most clamorous obstinacy to any support which they think essential to their existence; and to the miserable and impoverished, every encroachment, however small, seems to threaten destruction. This principle, whilst it accounts for the litigious subtlety of the "wildest of the Irish," unites with the former in the case of the Hindoos of the present day; than whom a more wretched and oppressed race is probably not to be found on the face of the earth.

In like manner, the extremely artificial nature of their social system has rendered the Hindoos obnoxious to several other reproaches, which the impressions of the moment, rather than calm observation, has induced some writers to vent against them. The laws of Menu appear to have considered the whole frame of society simply as an aggregate of family circles, the extent of which was accurately ascertained by the ties of consanguinity. It was incumbent upon each head of a family to attend to every call for support made by any of his kindred, and as long as an individual remained with his blood relations, he shared their last mouthful of subsistence. When, however, a Hindoo wandered from his home, and happened to be reduced to distress, the same arrangement which had secured him from want, now prevented his receiving assistance from strangers; he was looked upon as an outcast—as a man who had no connexions nor claims upon society; or, what was worse, he might have forfeited them by misconduct. To him the feast of nature was literally full, and those sitting at the table were only astonished that he should endeavour to intrude himself amongst them; whilst, too, they were already crowded perhaps beyond their competence, in addition to the alms which they were expected to bestow upon a ravenous priesthood.

The last charge, however, the want of personal courage, is of a graver nature than any of the others; and as a belief in its truth is calculated to act injuriously upon the line of policy adopted by our Government, it may not be improper to investigate it more minutely.

The foundation of this charge is doubtless the apparent ease with which Hindostan has so frequently been subdued; but when we enquire into the circumstances attending its subjugation by the Arab, or Saracen, and Tartar hordes, we find that the success of those invaders depended upon very different, and, indeed, opposite principles, from those of all subsequent assailants. In the army of Mamhoud, numbers and physical strength were aided by religious enthusiasm; and the inhabitants of Hindostan were too much divided amongst themselves, to be able to collect so large an army as that by which they were invaded; composed, as it was, of a hardy race of men inured to conquest, rapid in their movements, and cruel, even to extermination, when obstinately resisted. Such a description of warriors, continually recruited from their native hordes, were fully adequate to the conquest of any country; and without any impeachment of the natural courage of the Hindoos, it is not surprising that they felt before the same union of fanaticism and martial ardour, which the greater part of the civilized world was at that period unable to resist.

Still the efforts of the Hindoos to make head

against Mohammedan oppression were highly creditable to them; and it was not till the Affghan invasion, about two hundred years after the first attack, that the followers of the Prophet may be said to have gained a permanent footing in Hindostan. From that period the main struggle seems rather to have been amongst the Mohammedans themselves, than between the Mohammedans and Hindoos; though the latter we always find maintaining their independence in Rajpootanah, and in the strong country towards the centre of India, and occasionally taking advantage of existing commotions to enlarge their territory. Ultimately, however, the Hindoos, after a resistance of more than five centuries in duration, appear to have been completely overwhelmed. The Mohammedans, by degrees, formed a considerable portion of the population of the country; and, as a tribe addicted almost exclusively to the use of arms, and united by one common feeling of religious enthusiasm, they were amply sufficient to keep the rest of the community in subjection, when depressed and impoverished by continued exaction and arbitrary treatment. Mohammedan dynasties were established in various parts of the country, and foreign invaders, in addition to the superior discipline which their armies now began to display, were always certain of a considerable party in their interest, though always disposed to make common cause against the Hindoos upon any serious alarm of their encreasing strength. Nor were these alarms unfrequent. The exploits of the Mahrattas, in their unequal struggle with the Moguls, when the power of the latter was at its height, were sufficient to keep the whole force of the empire in check. And subsequently, the invasion of the Affghans (or Durannies) is alone supposed to have prevented the Mussulmans from being entirely driven out of Hindostan. In our own times, too, the same Hindoo power was so formidable as to induce the Government of Madras to evade the performance of their treaty with Hyder in 1769, and to expose their ally to destruction rather than provoke its hostility; the Bengal government, in 1765, having set them the example, by reinstating the Nabob of Oude in his territories, in order that they might be made a barrier to protect the dominions of the Company from the encroachments of those active and enterprising freebooters.

But the assaults of European powers were conducted upon totally different principles from those of the Mohammedan conquerors of India. Instead of numbers and superior ferocity, we see nothing but discipline and intellectual power— the arts of military combination, and attack and defence, were those alone which enabled so small a number of individuals to achieve such mighty triumphs. The Hindoos, accustomed to the dominion of their haughty liege lords, the Mohammedans, were struck with surprise on seeing the apparent ease with which the latter were discomfited; and they were therefore disposed to pay the greater respect to the heroic strangers: but to argue thence, that they were totally deficient in natural courage, is to commit a mistake that may eventually lead to the most disastrous consequences. When the wonderful exploits of Pecheco were yet fresh in the memory of the Portuguese, one of their leaders, the Marshal Don Fernando Cotigno, who, in conjunction with Alphonso Albuquerque, conducted the expedition against Calicut, made so lightly of the enterprise, that he advanced to the assault without armour, and with no other weapon than his walking-cane: when, his conduct, no doubt, influencing that of his soldiers, being attacked with spirit by the natives, he was completely defeated—his life, and that of many of his men becoming forfeit to his temerity, and the remainder of his troops being alone extricated by the able conduct of Albuquerque, who was himself wounded in the engagement. The military history of India is full of such examples.

Courage, though undoubtedly susceptible of considerable modification by the effect of political institutions, or even local peculiarities, is yet in some form or other common to every nation and climate; but it is the business of the philosopher to unfold and discriminate the various modes in which it is manifested. On close investigation it might be found, that, like the outward expression of grief in many countries, it depended upon certain forms and precepts, of an antiquity too remote to admit of satisfactory elucidation. Nothing can be so singular, and indeed revolting to the feelings of a man of refinement, as the apparently conventional mode in which it is customary with many nations, and particularly in Asia, to lament the decease of the nearest and dearest relations; and although a knowledge of ancient history ought to have prepared the mind of a well-educated European for this and many other peculiarities, yet such is the irresistible force of national prepossessions, that many are led to infer an almost total absence of the kindly affections amongst a people so characterised; forgetting, that to this very people our manners, under similar circumstances, must bear an equally singular appearance. The slightest degree of reflection, indeed, is sufficient to convince us that such an opinion is a gross libel upon human nature; and that, whatever may be the methods taken to express their feelings, the ties of love and affection, when torn asunder, occasion sensations of as much tenderness, and pangs as acute, in the breast of the untutored savage, as in that of civilized man. That the case is in some degree the same with natural courage, there are many reasons for believing, when we compare this faculty as it is evinced by different nations, or by individuals of the same nation, under different circumstances. Whatever may be the varieties of temperament, all, when the proper chord is touched, evince the same emotion, the same inherent spirit, and the same temporary disregard of personal ease and security.

It is not, then, the actual possession of courage, but the peculiar manifestation of it, which distinguishes one state of society from another. With the Hindoos it partakes of those restrictions with which their religious system seems to overlay all their natural powers; and in highly-civilized life, it is under the strict regulation of reflection and the sentiment of honour. In both cases, however, it acknowledges in reality an artificial standard; and instances of intrepidity, which are to be met with in savage life, occasionally surpass them both. As a natural characteristic, it is alone capable of being rendered of service to the state by discipline; which is, in fact, to courage, what civil Government is to liberty—it is an union of the courage of the whole body with the least possible sacrifice of the courage of the individual—the active intrepidity of the individual is repressed, in order to secure the greatest possible effect from a combination of that of the whole. Though its theory is essentially defensive, it is capable of any impulse of attack—it pushes forward and dilates itself, where opposition has been overcome, but rallies and collects its might when actually assailed—it provokes attack in the first instance, and, having repelled it, explodes, as it were, and completely overwhelms its adversaries. It is its defensive quality which ensures its triumph over unregulated courage, however heroic: for courage* is that faculty of mind, which prompts to deeds of hazard, under the probability that success will crown its exertions; all beyond this is self-devotion—an act which is very rarely called for under the most exalted patriotism. Discipline, however, by holding out little chance of success to its assailants, appears to demand nothing short of self-devotion to oppose it effectual-

* "Fortitudo est virtus pericula justa contemnens—munimentum humanæ imbecilitatis inexpugnabile: quod qui circumdedit sibi, securus in hoc vitæ obsidione perdurat. Utitur enim suis viribus, suis telis."—Seneca Epist.

ly; and hence, if not always irresistible in attack, it is ever formidable in defence. Instances of masses precipitating themselves upon almost certain destruction, in order to overwhelm, rather than conquer their adversaries, might easily be selected, even in modern times—In the attack of the Bastillè, and also of the entrenchments of Jemappe, it may be said of the defenders, as it was of the three hundred Fabii,* they were slain, not overcome;—whilst, on the other hand, the resistance of the French when the Russians attempted to retake their position at Borodino, and of the English squares at Waterloo, are instances of the triumphs of defensive discipline, under the most trying circumstances. But still, discipline, like other institutions of civilized life, appears, to the intrepid but uninstructed barbarian, to partake of pusillanimity; nor can he without difficulty persuade himself, that men of any real spirit could be brought to submit to such restraints. Acknowledging no other test of power than strength and intrepidity, when they contemplate their enemies as men differing in little or nothing, as to natural appearance, from themselves, they consi-

* "Ideò nemo trecentos Fabios victos dicit, sed occisos. Et Regulus captus est à Pœnis, non victus: et quisquis alius sævientis fortunæ vi ac pondere oppressus, non submittit animum."—Seneca.

der an organized body of them as merely containing the aggregate strength of the number of men composing it, without referring to the principles upon which their union is cemented. On the contrary, their huddling together, as it were, has all the appearance of fear; and the adventurous barbarian is only the more inclined to attack them. The Mamelukes of Egypt advanced to the muzzles of the French muskets, and, in their rage * at being unable to break the ranks, threw themselves from their horses, and seized the bayonets with their hands. The Lesghis, and other Tartars, cannot be brought to comprehend the nature of discipline; but in contempt of foot soldiers, threw themselves upon the Russian battalions with unabated confidence, notwithstanding their repeated discomfiture: they attribute the success even of the Russian artillery to the horses that draw it. The Nepaulese prisoners could not understand how their troops, accustomed to victory, had been beaten; and repeatedly said, "Give us Buctower

* It affords a remarkable illustration of the tendency which extremes have to meet under all circumstances, that the highly-disciplined Cuirassiers of the French army, notwithstanding the extensive experience which they must have had, displayed the same feeling of indignant surprise on being repulsed by the British squares on the heights of Mont St. Jean, as the Mamelukes of Egypt did when they were unable to penetrate the ranks of the French at the battle of the Pyramids.—See *Scott's Life of Napoleon*.

Thapa (one of their bravest chiefs) to command us, and we will fight it over again with you whenever you please;"—and the Burmese, it is well known, were so struck with the slender make of the Madras Sepoys, that they were convinced we owed our success to some peculiar quality possessed by the Europeans, and always said, that if the latter were withdrawn, they would drive the rest of the army into the sea.

It is, however, to take a very confined view of discipline, to suppose that it consists in nothing more than ranging men in even files, clothing them uniformly, and arming them with muskets, &c.;—all this may be done, and yet fail to inspire that confidence which is requisite to make good soldiers. Confidence, in this sense, is no less the result of the character of the Government itself, than of the personal weight of the commander, whether of a battalion, division, or army—the latter having, doubtless, the greatest influence in the hour of battle, but the former giving to the army its general qualifications and efficiency. Let any one observe the difficulty of keeping up the spirit and discipline of an army, when supplies are irregularly or scantly forwarded to it, or when good quarters and accommodation for the sick are not well attended to; and he will easily comprehend how much greater the influence of Government is, than any other. The feeling of security which the soldier experiences on being assured of the stability of the system under which he serves, and under the operation of which he expects to be provided for, when disabled, or worn out in the service, is so indispensable in upholding his firm attachment, that it has been observed, that in India the East India Company suffers in the opinion of the native troops, as well as of the inhabitants at large, from the vicarious nature of its Government. Known throughout the provinces chiefly as the collectors of the revenue, its agents or functionaries are expected to take their flight upon the appearance of any more formidable competition. The idea of a change of masters thus necessarily becomes familiar to the native army, and other classes of the community; and every report of the Company's reign being over, as Bishop Heber relates, displays the little moral influence which the dominion of a century has established over the minds of the people of Hindostan. The English are, in fact, considered in no other light than those foreigners who trained the Mahratta troops in the European manner, but who, neglecting to secure those guarantees of the permanence of their system, just alluded to, did but cripple the nations of those active marauders, and deliver them, chained and bound, into our hands—they gave them the cumbrous qualities of our tactics, which rendered it impossible for them to avoid coming in contact with our regular forces, but were unable to supply that confidence in their new organization which alone could give it effect, and enable them to contend with so formidable an antagonist. But this error, though obvious enough in the instance before us, we shall ourselves be in danger of committing, if we measure our strength merely by the number of men enrolled beneath our banners, without taking the necessary steps to inspire them with confidence in the stability of our power, grounded upon the general attachment of the people to our system of Government.*

* This observation applies with still greater force to the attempts lately made to introduce the system of European discipline amongst the Persians. Discipline, to be efficient, should be national;—until regular institutions afford a firm basis to rest upon, a reserve and rallying point in case of defeat, it is in vain to expect any permanent benefit from the adoption of the mere outward forms of European warfare. On the contrary, the experiment will be attended with the manifest disadvantage of forcing the Persians into contact with more experienced soldiers, without holding out that prospect of renewed effort, even after repulse, which constitutes the redeeming characteristic of undisciplined valour. When men are once accustomed to act in concert, defeat and dispersion are generally fatal to them; they can no longer unite without the presence and assistance of some superior authority to re-organize them; their habits of regular discipline unfit them for the display of indi-

One point generally overlooked in appreciating the strength of our position in India, is, that the Mohammedans, besides the immense numbers that

vidual prowess; and whilst the more irregular bands of warriors are broken and dispersed only to unite again and combat with a keener thirst for revenge, the disciplined body, unless supported by a widely-extended system, having the confidence of the nation for its basis, is thrown into inextricable confusion, unable to rally till at a distance from the field of battle and safe from the attack of the enemy. It may, indeed, be objected, that great captains have, in all ages, kept their armies together by means of their own energy, unsupported by any ulterior system; but in these cases we shall find that, besides the more indiscriminate right of plunder, almost unknown in modern warfare, their discipline was enforced by the assistance of select bands, or reserves, which, whilst they formed a rallying point for those who were repulsed, kept the wavering in their ranks by the influence as much of fear as of example. In the cases before us, however,—the Mahrattas under the guidance of French officers, and the Persians under our own,—these reserves, which should be the support of the whole army, are thrown forward in the commencement of the conflict, and, being once beaten, there is no longer any hope of opposing the progress of the enemy. The declaration of Aga Mahomed Khan,* that he knew better than to run his head against the Russian walls of steel, and expose his irregular army to be destroyed by their cannon and disciplined troops, was exactly to the point. "Their shot," said the sagacious monarch, "shall never reach me; but they shall possess no country beyond its range; they shall not know sleep; and let them

* Sketches in Persia, chapter xx.

settled in Hindostan on each of their three grand irruptions, received constant accessions to their strength by Mussulman adventurers of all coun-

march where they choose, I will surround them with a desert." This observation reminds us of the advice of Memnon the Rhodian, for conducting the war against Alexander the Great, as given by *Diodorus Siculus and Arrian,†—to check the Macedonians by destroying the country before them, and preventing their marching forward for want of provisions; to trample the herbage under their horses' feet; to burn the produce of the country, and even to lay the towns and villages waste; "by which means," says the latter, "Alexander, finding himself destitute of provision and forage, would be unable to penetrate farther." To the portion of this opinion on the inexpediency of forming the Persians into regular battalions, Sir John Malcolm seems to have given his ready assent; though, from what is stated in the chapter immediately preceding the one first quoted, not altogether upon very correct principles; for, if the harlequin-changes which are there referred to, had indeed left his Persian friends no remains of barbarism but their beards, the introduction of the modern system of discipline would be in all respects right and proper; it would then be the effect of an efficient cause:—it is only its premature introduction before other departments of the state, and indeed the nation generally, had been sufficiently improved to enable them to appreciate its value, and to give it full effect, that is earnestly to be deprecated. If they go hand in hand with civilization, there is plenty of good stuff in Persia to oppose the progress of the Russians; but by no other means is this desirable end to be effected.

* Lib. xvii. c. 2. † Lib. i. c. 13.

tries, whether from the North, or by the Indian Ocean and Persian Gulf. It was by this extensive colonization that their numbers were augmented beyond the usual ratio of natural increase, and their spirit was enabled to keep pace with that of their sect in other parts of the world; a point which, though it appear of easy accomplishment to us, was sufficient to preserve their intellectual superiority over the degraded Hindoo, as well as to give them great weight as a component part of the population. To this state of things our present situation bears no sort of resemblance, nor is there indeed any thing strictly analogous in all history to the conquest of Hindostan by our countrymen. All other extensive conquests have been effected by means of large armies, and maintained either by such armies settling in the conquered country, or protecting the settlement of their fellow countrymen.* But in India, the number of European troops employed at any one period, has been inconceivably small; and our acquisitions have at once been made and maintained almost entirely by the agency of our conquered subjects. At the decisive battle of Plassey, Lord

* See a long enumeration of instances given by Seneca, ending with the passage quoted by Gibbon, (Decline and Fall, chap. ii.) "Wheresoever the Roman conquers, he inhabits."

Clive had only nine hundred Europeans; and at the present day, the number of Europeans in the whole army is not more than as one to ten native soldiers. The Europeans of every description, actually in India, are only in the proportion of one to three thousand natives; whilst under the height of the Mogul government, the Mohammedans are said never to have been less than one-twentieth, though sometimes estimated as high as one-twelfth of the whole population.

With this immense disparity of numbers against us, it is surely unwise, and even criminal, to shut our eyes to the real circumstances by which our situation, as the ruling caste of India, is distinguished. If, indeed, our hold upon the natives is in opinion—if they look up to us with confidence for security of person and property, as well as for encouragement in whatever conduces to their happiness and prosperity—which, indeed, is the only rational meaning of an empire of opinion—then it behoves us to endeavour, by every means in our power, to diffuse the benefits of education throughout the country; to reform the habits of the people; to excite their industry, and to impress them with that consciousness of their own defects, which shall at once awaken in them the desire of knowledge, and dispose them to rely upon the wisdom and beneficent intentions of their rulers. But if by opinion, it is meant to be insinuated, as is sometimes the case, that our strength depends upon the ignorance of the natives of their immense numerical preponderance, then the idea displays not only the extreme of folly, and inattention to passing events,* but is in itself highly dangerous to the continuance of our rule. That ignorance, even if it exist at present, cannot possibly be expected to endure much longer; and if in the mean time any serious danger threaten

* The opposition to the house-tax, &c. at Benares and Bareilly—and lately, the disaffection manifested throughout the provinces during the whole period of the Burmese war—but particularly on the siege of Burtpore being undertaken, are well known. A long catalogue of the signs of the times, more than sufficient under a military despotism and an enslaved press to indicate the temper of the people, might easily be prepared;—two only are here selected. In a late disturbance in the South of India, when a distinguished servant of the Company lost his life, the natives are said to have cut off his right hand, and nailed it to the gate of their fortress, with an inscription, purporting that it belonged to one who had boasted that he never returned a native's salute. In Calcutta, under the eye of the Supreme Government, a wealthy Hindoo, who had erected an immense bazar at an enormous expense, on speculation, was almost ruined by the steady and unanimous refusal of the natives to resort to it, because he was said to have entered into a contract for the purchase of Government salt, by which the already high price of that article was likely to be farther enhanced.

our dominion, the natives will not fail to ask themselves, how far it is desirable to make common cause with a nation which has shown so little solicitude for their welfare. The presence of a rival power will at least afford them the prospect of a change; and as to the great mass of the population of Hindostan no change could well be for the worse, we ought not to be surprised at any excesses into which they may be driven. For nations do not, like individuals, "rather bear the ills they have than fly to others which they know not of;" on the contrary, they strenuously exert themselves to get rid of the burthens which they feel to be galling and troublesome; and when their condition, notwithstanding all their efforts, is perceptibly deteriorating, they eagerly catch at any, even the most remote prospect of relief; they become desperate, and judge that, happen what may, they cannot be worse: by perpetually brooding over the possible evils of a revolution, they familiarize their imagination with disasters and dangers of every description; and it has been truly said, that he who despises life is inaccessible to pity, and that there is no enemy more truly formidable than one who is prepared to die.

## CHAPTER V.

### ON THE COLONIZATION OF INDIA.

"Instat enim et urget, et quo te cunque verteris, persequitur."

THAT the people of India are, generally speaking, immersed in almost hopeless poverty; that they have in fact nothing to lose, and every thing to gain by a change of masters; and that they must in consequence be quite indifferent to our weal or woe, in the event of danger threatening our dominion, must be quite evident to all who have attentively considered the three great features of our Indian revenue system: the effects which followed, and those which still continue to follow, upon the permanent settlement; the acknowledged aim and end of the Munro system, which is to tax industry and improvement, and to enable Government to drain all the surplus earnings of the cultivators, as the zemindars are allowed to do in Bengal; and lastly, the refusal on the part of the Court of Directors to grant any settlement to the ceded and conquered provinces, by which a limit may be affixed to the demands of the state upon the produce of the soil. In 1786, Mr. T. Grant thus describes the condition of the Hindoo peasantry: "A seer of rice with a little seasoning, a rag, a hut, or the canopy of heaven, (the whole brought within the daily expenditure of an anna, or twopence for each individual,) satisfy all the natural wants of an Hindostanny husbandman or manufacturer; and if he can save at the end of the year a couple of rupees from the produce of his industry, rated at one hundred in the market, he is infinitely richer, more contented, and easy in his circumstances, than the individual following either of these trades in England, who, after incurring a personal expense of two shillings a day, should be able to lay by an annual profit of two guineas from his whole estimated work of one hundred." Twenty-seven years afterwards, Warren Hastings, in his reply to a question put to him by Parliament, says: "The poor of India, who are the people, have no*

* One might imagine that with these gentlemen, to want nothing, and to want every thing, were synonymous expressions. Much general misapprehension prevails in England respecting the actual wants of the people of India: when we read of the rag which covers the lower classes, and the fine cloth in which the wealthy are wrapped, we think only of the blessing of living in so genial a clime, forgetting

wants; unless the scanty rags which they wear, their huts, and simple food may be considered as such, and these they have upon the ground which they tread upon." And in Mr. Tucker's late work on the Finances of the Company, the following is the description given: "The habits of the great body of the people are simple and uniform; their diet is spare, and confined generally to a few articles of the first necessity—rice, vegetables, fish, and the smaller grains; their clothing is scanty and mean; their habitations poor and unfurnished; what we term luxuries, are confined to the opulent few. Capital is thinly distributed over the surface; and even the advantages of a genial climate, a prolific soil, and of manufacturing skill, were not found sufficient to swell the stream of commerce. In all this the keen eye of the financier could see nothing to touch; the objects were too minute and worthless,* &c." Thus

that the temperature varies from forty to fifty degrees of Farenheit's thermometer during the year, and, not unfrequently, fifteen or twenty degrees during twenty-four hours. So far, indeed, from clothing being unnecessary, there are perhaps few countries in which the poor suffer more from the want of it; even in the hot weather, the same poverty which puts clothing out of their reach, deprives them of oil, without which their sufferings from a scorching sun are excessive.

* "Review of Financial State," &c. p. 49. It is worthy of

we see, that, at this moment, the account of the poverty of the inhabitants, given, too, by men who

remark, that, notwithstanding the worthless and minute nature of the objects of taxation here apparently assigned as a reason for the immense land-tax of India, other taxes formed, at the period of Mr. Tucker's writing, more than a moiety of the whole revenue of the Bengal Presidency. The salt monopoly, in particular, yields two-thirds as much as the land-revenue of the lower provinces; approaching, as Mr. Tucker himself expresses it, to a poll-tax of no trifling amount. The price of salt Mr. T. states to be about 12½ pence per annum to the consumers, for six seers, (which, however, is but a small average allowance;) but as he inadvertently grounds his estimate upon the wholesale price obtained by Government, it is obviously too low. And, in point of fact, the retail price is always as high as two annas per seer, which will raise the expenditure of each individual to eighteen pence, instead of twelve pence half-penny, or about 50 per cent. upon the wholesale price: which, assuming Mr. T.'s estimate of natural price to be correct, (about one-third the gross sale price,) will make the amount of tax to Government, on account of salt, about one shilling, instead of eight pence halfpenny a head per annum, as he has stated it. This computation agrees, also, with the amount of gross sales and charges given in Mr. Prinsep's financial result of Lord Hastings' administration. The charge of 55,53,176 rupees being deducted from 2,04,75,412 rupees, and the remainder divided by thirty millions, the supposed amount of population, gives 11.925 pence, or very nearly one shilling; which, being taken as the amount of poll-tax received by Government, and 50 per cent. added for the advance of retail price, gives about eighteen pence a head, as before. Independent of this tax, the customs,

ranked amongst the firmest advocates of the Company, applies with as much force as it did nearly half a century ago, notwithstanding the boasted good effects of our rule. Yet more than thirty-five years have now elapsed since the commencement of the discussion respecting the introduction of a more equitable relation between landlord and tenant, upon the model of European tenures, and the subject is still apparently as far as ever from being set at rest. Whole volumes have been written upon the condition of our Eastern possessions, but nothing whatever has been done towards the removal of those causes which weigh down the spirit, and paralyze the exertions, of the great mass of their population. In the interminable controversy, one party accuses the other of exclusively employing the reasoning dictated by European prepossessions, whilst the other retorts the reproach of Orientalism upon all those who would

stamps, and excise, bear with considerable weight upon the people of India: though their consumption of taxable objects may be small, the general rise of prices, occasioned by high taxation, reaches all classes; for the imposition of a tax is like the casting of a stone into the water—the greatest agitation occurs in the first instance at the spot where it falls, but the movement thus occasioned soon subsides, and is carried in circling eddies to the very margin of the pool, leaving its surface smooth and undisturbed, but raised in its level exactly in proportion to the size of the body thrown into it.

persuade the world that the Indian Government ought to follow in the steps of their Mohammedan predecessors; but it must be allowed, that if there is little of unquestionable wisdom in the institutions even of the most enlightened of the old states of Europe, there is certainly infinitely less that is worthy of imitation to be found in the most recondite maxims of Asiatic government. In the mean time, however, whilst we deliberate, the enemy is almost at our gates, and the only opportunity we shall probably ever possess of increasing our moral strength, and organising our resources, is irretrievably passing away.

Whatever notions, abstract or practical, may form the plan upon which the Indian Government, if sincerely desirous to improve the condition of the country, may think proper to act—and, as has before been observed, there is reason to believe, that any system founded upon natural equity and the sound principles of common sense would speedily approve itself to the understandings, and even to the prejudices of the natives—it is quite evident that, without a great change in the present circumstances of society, there would be no adequate foundation for it to rest upon. The people whom we govern are swayed by social and religious institutions, which seem framed for the express purpose of keeping them in perpetual non-age; and as long as those institutions continue to be unshaken by education and example, it is needless to expect that any desire of improvement will be evinced, or any encouragement be given for hoping that they will profit by the endeavours made to ameliorate their condition. Where ignorance, poverty, and superstition, are all combined, the case may well appear hopeless to those who shrink from the trouble and responsibility of effecting or recommending any alteration in the settled order of things, that is not in a manner forced upon their adoption by the resistless, though often tedious advance of practical knowledge. With the Hindoos, that advance must be even more effectually impeded by their poverty than by their ignorance and superstition. The degree of skill to be acquired in the course of laborious occupations, under the pressure of great poverty, is unavoidably small: if it be true that necessity is the mother of invention, it is no less so that her bantling will never come to maturity unless she have strength and leisure to nurse it. In order to give effect to the happy thoughts which are sometimes struck out on the emergency of the occasion, some spare time is required for reflection and experiment. Knowledge is power in every sense; but practical is not speculative knowledge, and both are requisite in order to mature the sudden conceptions of genius, when acted upon by necessity. There can be no doubt that many useful discoveries are lost to society for want of time to record and consolidate them; and it is possible that the institution of castes and hereditary trades among the Hindoos, may have taken its rise from the idea, that constant application to one specific employment was favourable to that concentration of mind, which leads to invention and improvement. Cicero expresses himself to this effect in the treatise from which the motto to this chapter is taken;* and, indeed, before the discovery of the advantages to be derived from the division of labour, nothing short of the application of a whole life, accompanied by the traditional lights communicated from father to son, must have appeared sufficient to qualify an individual for the exercise of a distinct trade. The knowledge, which with us is communicated by means of books, must, in the rude times adverted to, have been imparted entirely by oral instruction and practical example; and each successive scholar, instead of enjoying the benefit of the accumulated experience of his predecessors in the art which he was anxious to acquire, and starting, as it were, from the landmarks which they had established, was obliged to conform to the

* "Affert autem vetustas omnibus in rebus longinquâ observatione incredibilem scientiam."—De Divinatione, i. 49.

same process, and to follow the same undeviating routine, which appeared to be the only secret of their superior dexterity.

Thus the ordinary duration of human life seemed too short to produce any material improvement; and accordingly, if the expertness with which the Hindoos manage the simple contrivances which alone are known to them, is, at first sight, calculated to excite the admiration of an European observer; that feeling, when analyzed, will be found to proceed rather from surprise at so much being effected by means apparently so inadequate, than from any impression of the actual knowledge displayed by the artist; and certainly, as far as the point can be ascertained, no material improvement in the arts has taken place amongst them for ages. In India, then, where the number of persons who are qualified to direct or assist in so great a work as the reformation of the habits and manners of a numerous population, is so small and fluctuating, the task is looked upon as quite impracticable.

The efforts that have been made by humane and enlightened individuals, to obtain a footing in this great sea of darkness, have often been interrupted, or entirely relinquished, for want of the proper means to secure and render permanent what they had gained; and before their efforts could be renewed with any prospect of success, the waves of ignorance and superstition have swept away all but the slight vestiges of their labours, which were discernible in the barbarous dialect, and not unfrequently in the dissolute manners of their former pupils and assistants in the generous undertaking. Nor is this the case in the work of education alone. In almost every other attempt, whether of Government or of individuals, there is the same character* of instability,

* These effects are especially visible on the site of old Government establishments, or indigo manufactories, which have been abandoned: there every thing seems invested with a sort of premature antiquity. In India, the decay and dilapidation of deserted buildings is astonishingly rapid, owing to the alternate dryness and humidity of the atmosphere, and the rank vegetation which quickly makes its appearance in every hole or crevice: this, together with the natural tendency of the great mass of the community to absorb and obliterate the slender alteration, either in language or customs, which the short residence of Europeans may have produced, almost induces the observer to imagine that he is surveying the ruins of some centuries, instead of those of an establishment but a few years deserted. Here, the feeble remains of some English terms appear as if transmitted by tradition beyond the memory of living man. There, a few implements, or a piece of broken furniture, the uses of which have already become nearly obsolete; or, it may be, some remains of superiority in the draught, or axletree of the carts, or *hackerries*, of the vicinity, proclaim the former existence of a better

the same want of consistent and persevering advances towards a definite end, in consequence of

state of things; but from the imperfect traces still discernible, the date appears almost to baffle enquiry. In like manner, the improvements which the occasional residence of Europeans may have effected in the natural products of the soil, linger but a few years after the departure of the individuals who introduced them: thus the fruits and vegetables of a neighbourhood tenanted by European gentlemen, being an object of profit, retain a considerable celebrity for a comparatively longer period, but in the end merge into the general mass of wild and uncultivated produce. Thus several parts of the country, which a few years since were famed for producing good mangoes, peaches, plantains, &c. no longer furnish any but the common sort; and, in general, the fruit may be said to grow almost wild, excepting on a few spots in the actual occupation of Europeans, or but recently abandoned by them. Of these a great number are susceptible of very considerable improvement; and, with care and attention, might be made to equal the produce of any climate on the globe.

Amongst the means by which settlements might be effected, and improvements in the useful arts rendered permanent, the establishment of Moravian missions, upon tracts of Government land, in different parts of the country, deserves to be mentioned. From their unobtrusive habits, and from the actual conversion of the natives forming no part of their object, though they are at all times willing to receive such as voluntarily join their communion, this most useful sect seems admirably fitted for setting an example to the people of Hindostan, of the benefit of moral conduct, in conjunction with peaceful and industrious habits of life.

the frequent changes which occur amongst the persons to whom the execution of any project requiring time and assiduity is entrusted. India, indeed, as a field of exertion for an intelligent, well-informed, and industrious class of men, may be said to be almost entirely fallow and uncultivated: a teeming soil is tilled much in the same manner as a school-boy prepares his little plot for mustard and cress.

Works of labour are performed by the effort of mere numbers, with scarcely any, even the rudest application of mechanical contrivance: the implements made use of are all of the coarsest and most cumbrous description; and these, in the feeble hands of the listless and indolent beings who wield them, are, for the most part, so useless, that a crowd of labourers in any one line of industry, will scarcely execute more work than two or three able-bodied Europeans. Thus, whilst labour is nominally cheap, and actually so, as far as relates to the poor wretches themselves, it is, in reality, extravagantly high to those who employ them. Improvements to be seen in the great establishments and work-yards of Calcutta, and other cities, and wherever, in short, there are Europeans to direct and superintend the native workmen, have led many to imagine the latter more expert and intelligent than is the fact: but these good symptoms are confined to the immediate vicinity of the establishments adverted to; and, like all other sorts of instruction, communicated under present circumstances, are exceedingly transient in their effects, and liable to disappear with the removal of the cause which gave them birth. In short, every Englishman who has been much in the interior of India is sensible of the slowness and want of common knowledge of unassisted native workmen, and of the helplessness to which his countrymen are reduced when planted amidst such a population; and yet, when it is proposed to give a better direction to native industry, by supplying it with examples and instruction upon fixed and durable principles, we hear nothing but of the difficulty and inutility of the measure.

The measure so often suggested, and so often evaded, or overruled, is Colonization. To counteract the disadvantages under which all classes of the community at present labour, to confer a benefit upon the governors, no less than upon the governed, Colonization is the only plan that can be adopted with any prospect of success.

By the adoption of this measure,* in respect to

* "Our empire there," (in India,) observes Sir John Malcolm, "has already derived, and must continue to derive,

India, it is not meant that a crowd of settlers should be sent out as they are to the Cape of Good Hope, Canada, or Van Diemen's Land. Colonization is, in fact, of two distinct kinds, cor-

the greatest benefit from the enterprise of British merchants, which has diffused wealth, encouraged industry, and promoted the general prosperity of the country; adding, by the increase of its resources, to the strength of the Government. English artisans have also, within a narrower sphere, been most useful: neither of these classes here, in any way, come in collision with our native subjects, by trenching upon their right of claims; on the contrary, they have been their benefactors; they have given them an example of the benefits that accrue to individuals and nations from large and liberal principles of trade; they have taught them the useful and ornamental arts of life, and it is to them that we must chiefly look, as affording examples for the natives to follow in every improvement of civilized society."—*Pol. Hist.* vol. ii. p. 255. —No testimony in favour of Colonization can well be stronger than this; and yet the General, afterwards, observing that English merchants and artisans had established manufactories in provinces which had been long under our rule, states it as his opinion, that " many reasons concur to make the increase of these settlers impolitic." What these reasons are, however, he does not condescend to inform us. But this is only one of those instances of hot and cold being blown upon the same subject with which the Political History abounds. Another instance, from the same chapter, may here be given. Speaking of the Anglo-Indians, he says, " A just and generous Government will not, however, have recourse to that narrow principle which apportions benefits by the power any class of its subjects have of enforcing them;

responding with the state of the country which sends forth the colonists, as well as of that which receives them. One is intended for the benefit of the former, which relieves itself by encouraging

nor will it withhold any reasonable boons, because it is offended by the temper in which they are solicited. Acting on different grounds, it will give to this, as to every other class of its subjects, that consideration which is due to their condition, and which will fill their reasonable hopes, without a sacrifice of any essential interest of the empire. Though placed under circumstances of depression and discouragement, this body of men has lost few opportunities of becoming useful and respected in the different walks of life to which their pursuits have been directed. We should continue, therefore, to cultivate their moral and religious principles; and whilst we institute and encourage seminaries for their instruction upon an extended scale, we should provide the means of their future employment, in the condition of life best suited to their respective situations and qualifications." Who would not suppose from this that the writer was about to propose that education and character should furnish the criterion of fitness for employment by the state, for this class, as well as for any other of the Christian community of India; but no: Sir John goes on to observe, that, "if the justice of his proposition is admitted, the means of carrying it into execution will not be difficult, as they require *no change in those salutary restraints*, in which the principles of both the civil and military services in India are now grounded." And what are these principles of salutary restraint but the *positive exclusion* of the class, whose interest he thus affects to espouse, from both the civil and military branches of the service!—This, and several other passages of the work, exhibiting the

the emigration of its surplus population; the other is for the benefit of the latter, and consists in the infusion of intelligence and activity into the social mass, by the settlement of men of skill, industry, and capital. It is precisely this infusion, this admixture of men of energy and intelligence, with its already numerous, but almost torpid population, which is required for Hindostan, to set before the inhabitants the effects which so fine a climate is capable of producing, when their industry * is

struggle of a good and evil principle, have led many to believe that it was originally written in one frame of mind, and afterwards retouched and prepared for publication in another.

* Amongst those who have formed, or rather, who have been industrious in inculcating an erroneous impression of the mode in which it is proposed to extend the principle of Colonization to India, is Sir John Malcolm. He commences (*Political History*, vol. ii. p. 250,) by telling his readers, that no extensive colonization can take place, unless the settlers are admitted to have property in the soil: and then goes on to say, that " the grounds upon which the impolicy and danger of admitting Englishmen to follow agricultural pursuits in India rest, are, in a great degree, referable to the peculiar nature of our Eastern possessions, which must never be viewed as a colony." This proposition is what logicians call identical, and amounts to this:—India must never be colonized, because it must never be viewed as a colony. He does not give any reason why Colonization should not be permitted, other than by informing us, that whilst we have guaranteed to our subjects the enjoyment of their property, laws, usages, and religion, we ought to impart such improvement

directed with ability, and animated by an active and independent spirit.

The general advantages attendant upon this great measure will not be confined to the natives alone, or to the working classes; the Government of the country will feel the benefit of it in almost

as will promote their happiness, and the general prosperity of the country; but not to associate with our improvement any measure, of which the operation is likely to interfere with their interest, to offend their prejudices, or to outrage their cherished habits and sentiments;" by which insidious *petitio principii*, he plainly insinuates, that Colonization would inevitably work all the mischief alluded to. He afterwards admits, however, (p. 251.) that land might be purchased, "where our regulations have made it saleable;" and thus unwarily affords us a clue to his whole argument upon this subject; for, on enquiring how it happens that the property of the natives is not everywhere saleable at the option of the possessor, we are naturally reminded that a permanent settlement, conferring the right of property in the soil, has, as yet, been given but to a small portion of the Company's dominions; and that, in all other parts of India, Government still claim and exercise the right of universal landlord. Sir John Malcolm's apparent solicitude, therefore, about the rights and cherished habits of the inhabitants of India, is but one of the many instances in which that writer makes use of certain set phrases, in order to "keep the word of promise to the ear, and break it to the hope." The only rights for which he contends, are those of the Company to have a share of the advantages resulting from the increased produce of the soil, no matter how that increase has been effected: in other

every stage of its administration; but more particularly in the check and restraint which the presence of respectable settlers will impose upon such of the public functionaries as are liable to be betrayed into the commission of acts of an arbitrary and unjustifiable nature, by the too great discre-

words, to tax the land to the utmost. In his account of the Bareilly insurrection, he is contented with slightly passing over the opinion of the Commission in favour of a permanent settlement of the Upper Provinces. In vol. ii. p. 169, he informs us, that the permanent settlement of 1789,—the only act of the Company which secures the right of property in the soil to any portion of their subjects,—"is now admitted, by its warmest advocates, to have been too much hurried," &c.; and, in page 183, we are told, that "a long period must still elapse before we have accumulated facts and experience, in which we can venture to establish permanent and unalterable arrangements;" and again, page 250, the impossibility of recalling the favours and concessions granted by the Company to its subjects, without impairing the confidence of the natives in the good faith of Government, is assigned as a reason that "no measures should be adopted *creative of such rights and privileges*, unless we have the clearest conviction that they can be permanently maintained, without injury or danger to our native subjects, and to the general interest of our empire of India." This sort of reasoning is the more extraordinary, as the writer, at page 173, had evinced a sounder knowledge of his subject, by observing, that "a government which precludes itself from any increase of territorial assessment, must look to the general diffusion of wealth for the future improvement of its resources; and though a long period

tion with which their distance from the seat of Government induces them to believe themselves armed, and in the assistance which such men would have it in their power to render the state, by acting in the commission of the peace, and relieving the magistrate of the district from a portion of his too extensive and often incompatible duties.

must elapse before it can venture to subject to direct taxation any of the possessors of that affluence which its liberal policy has created, it may expect to receive an early and constantly increasing return, through the enlarged demand for the necessary commodities and luxuries of life required for a population advancing in numbers and comfort, and the consequent progressive improvement of duties and customs." But thus it is throughout the work referred to. It was published, apparently, with a view of supporting what are termed the rights of the Company, grounded upon a recommendation to respect the barbarous customs and cherished habits and sentiments of the natives, together with an adherence to the usages of the governments in India which preceded our own—tolerably efficient barriers against the progress of civilization, it must be allowed!—Here and there, however, symptoms of a better spirit become apparent; but these only bubble to the surface of the stagnant mass, show themselves for an instant, then burst and disappear for ever. Sir John is, indeed, as he has elsewhere styled himself, "the advocate of *very slow* reform." He says, "we cannot interfere in the prevention of infanticide, or in the self-sacrifice of females on the funeral pile of their husbands, otherwise than by praise of those who abstain from such acts, and neglect of

The "brief authority" of public officers when exercised in situations remote from the capital, (and in Bengal the term *remote* may be applied to districts not very distant from Calcutta, in consequence of the * slowness and difficulty of communication between all stations excepting those lying on the principal military road, or in the direction of the stream of the great rivers, no less than in consequence of the total silence of an enslaved press upon all subjects relating to the ser-

those who approve or perpetrate them. How much more manly was the course pursued by Capt. Kennedy, the Political Agent at Subathoo: see that officer's Report on the State of the Hill Tribes entrusted to his superintendence:—see Calcutta Annual Register for 1821. A system of Jesuitical compromise is certainly not calculated to raise us in the estimation of that part of our Indian subjects whose good opinion is worth preserving.

* It is worthy of remark, that, notwithstanding the inconvenience experienced for want of the means of rapidly transmitting intelligence throughout India, the line of communication by telegraph, which was commenced more than eleven years ago, is not yet completed even half-way to Agra. It is calculated, that if this method of communicating with the frontier had been in operation at the period of the first armament against Burtpore, under the late Sir David Ochterlony, the state would have saved, on that occasion, in extraordinary expenses alone, as much as they have lavished upon that hitherto useless project during the eleven years of indecision above mentioned.

vants of Government,) and the excesses occasionally committed by individuals now residing by special favour in the country, and who may be disposed to avail themselves of their distance from the district, or city courts, and of the apparent credit which they enjoy with men in authority, as by the smallness of their numbers, and the habitual deference with which they are regarded by the submissive natives, would meet with a salutary check in the residence of a numerous and respectable class of their countrymen, and that mutual feeling of independence and consideration would be established, which is at once the cause and the effect of morality and upright conduct.

The temptation to make bad use of their power, wealth, or influence, is as great, and probably as mischievous in its effect, amongst the higher classes of natives themselves, as amongst Europeans. Natives of all ranks are prone to ill-treat those beneath them; and men of wealth and authority press servants and porters, and exact supplies of all kinds, on their own terms, without any apprehension of being called to account for so doing; for such is the difficulty of obtaining redress under such circumstances, both in regard to the actual expense of prosecuting in the first instance, and the great trouble and interruption of business intailed by an appeal to our courts, at the distance of sometimes more than an hundred miles, that very few can be found either rich or persevering enough to go through with the process.* In the present condition of the more wealthy classes of natives, in respect of moral feeling; and of the poorer classes, as to the contempt and helplessness into which they are fallen, no laws or prohibitions can be effectual in repressing the disorders adverted to; † and any advantage to be gained by associating individuals of rank in the administration of the provinces, would be greatly alloyed, by the danger to be apprehended from adding personal influence to the numerical preponderance already so fearfully on the side of the natives. A late member of the Calcutta Government is said to have been well aware of the great oppression practised by the darogahs, or subordinate police authorities, as well as by the munsiffs, or native civil commissioners, and to have recommended the abolishment of their appointments in favour of the zemindars, who were to have been

* As an instance, it may be mentioned that the jurisdiction of the Zillah Court of the twenty-four Pergunahs, in the neighbourhood of Calcutta, extends as far as the Island of Saugor, probably 120 miles.

† "Là dove la materia è corrotta," says Machiavelli, "le buone leggi non giovano."

vested with authority to investigate and decide upon civil and criminal complaints of a specified extent; but as there were few objections against one set of natives which did not apply with equal force to every other, the project appears to have been abandoned. The only method, indeed, which suggests itself for relieving Government from this twofold embarrassment, without increasing the number of their civil and military functionaries beyond the competence of their utmost revenues to support the expense of, is to permit and encourage the settlement of Europeans throughout the country, not only with a view of rendering their services available in carrying the laws into effect, but by reforming the habits and manners of the natives, and setting before them the spectacle of an industrious class of men, living under the same laws as themselves, enjoying the comforts and conveniences of life by the exertion of their skill and diligence, and a rigid adherence to the principles of morality and justice in the regulation of their concerns.

Many, however, are inclined to doubt how far the proposed settlers might promote the advantage of the under tenants and cultivators, under the system of landed property at present established in India. Whilst the profits of capital vested in land in England are acknowledged to be lower than by most other methods of employing it, ample compensation is supposed to be made by the advantage which the possession of real property confers, in the shape of political influence, votes in elections, eligibility for, or patronage of, local appointments, militia commissions, &c., together with game and other privileges; and the landlord is thereby disposed, not only to refrain from rack-renting his estate, but to grant occasional indulgences to his tenants, as circumstances may require. But in India no advantage is attached to the possession of land beyond the direct amount of its rent; the landholder looks upon the crop as his best security for the payment of his own dues and those of Government; and the vigilance which his intermediate position between the State and the cultivators of the soil obliges him to exert, has, as has been before observed, the most unfavourable effect upon the spirit and industry of the great bulk of the people. As long as this state of things is allowed to continue, it may be thought that the introduction of European settlers would fail to be attended with the benefit anticipated; for if they were to become landholders, their interests being in all respects the same as the present proprietors, they would have every temptation to bear as severely upon their under-tenants; and it would be some time before the effects of general improvement and encreased industry would introduce a more liberal mode of proceeding. The demand for produce of all kinds might, indeed, be expected shortly to encrease the aggregate industry of the country, and raise the value of labour; but in the mean time, to secure to the under-tenant and ryots as much as possible the advantages which, as holders of farms, they would not fail to derive from the encreased demand for land which an influx of capital would occasion, some provision on the part of Government appears desirable. Not that it is probable that, without a reform in the habits and manners of the people, any positive regulation will materially improve the condition of the two classes in question; but by giving them a firmer hold upon the land they cultivate, the present value of their rights would be enhanced, and they would in some measure be secured from the exactions of any new purchasers of the zemindary estates, of which their fields or farms constitute a portion. Notwithstanding every effort that can be made, the value of those rights will still be very small, and liable to constant diminution, by the rapid increase of population, which existing laws * in favour of marriage render inevi-

* The Mutsu Puran says, "No man ought to remain unmarried even for a day; if he does so, he must perform certain penances as an atonement; and this, although he may

table. These laws, which it is imperative upon every Hindoo to obey, must tend greatly to counteract every attempt which is made to improve the condition of the people; and until, by slow degrees, the energies of the country shall be completely roused, and a general demand for labour shall give every man the means of obtaining a livelihood in proportion to his intelligence and industry, no permanent amelioration can be expected. Meanwhile, however, by rescuing the small farmers, &c. from the situation of tenants at will,

otherwise be diligent in prayer, in giving alms, and in studying the Vedah." And the Bubusut Puran, "If a man marry after his forty-eighth year he shall be accounted sinful; but if he remain unmarried, or without a male child, until his forty-eighth year, all the good actions of his life shall be of no service to him." Again, the Chundogopurusistang—"A girl of ten years old is arrived at the age of puberty, therefore let her be given in marriage in the course of her tenth year." And in the Bubusut Puran, "If a girl is not married before the age of puberty, her father, mother, and eldest brother, are rendered for ever sinful."

Adverting to the great increase of population which laws of this nature must occasion, it may here be remarked, that the quantity of salt annually sold by the Government may form a criterion by which to judge of the general impoverishment of the people, or the degree in which they are inconvenienced by that cruel monopoly. On comparing the gross sales and selling prices of salt given in Mr. Tucker's Review of the Finances of the Company, pp. 54, 55, 56, the increase

liable to be sold, as it were, with the farms they occupy, without being sure of being allowed to hold them a day beyond the transfer, they will have an opportunity of profiting by any accidental acquisitions of means, or local convenience, which may arise; and be able to better their condition, without the constant apprehension of having the produce of their labour wrested from them.— "Agriculture," says the Lord Archon in the 'Oceana,' "is the bread of the nation; we are hung upon it by the teeth; it is a mighty nursery of strength; the best army; the most assured knapsack; it is managed with the least turbulent or

in the quantity supplied does not appear to bear any proportion to the supposed increase of population; the consequence is, that the price has been raised almost a hundred per cent. in a period of thirteen years; and whilst this increased demand, when the quantity produced has been augmented by about one-fifth, affords a satisfactory proof of the greater proportional increase in the population; it also serves to show how extensively the tax must operate as a grievance on the people, "whose simple diet requires the addition of salt as a stimulant." If there be truth in Mr. Tucker's estimate, the Company would at once increase their revenue, and diminish the inconveniences experienced by the people, if they were to augment the quantity of salt at least two-fold.

For an account of the oppressions suffered by the salt-manufacturers, scarcely surpassed by the *mita* of South America, see Rickards, p. 118. In 1825, Mr. Tucker says, "This grievance has, *I trust*, been removed."

ambitious, the most innocent hands of all other arts—wherefore I am of Aristotle's opinion, that a commonwealth of husbandmen, and such as ours, must be the best of all others. I wish I were husband good enough to direct something to this end: but racking of rents is a vile thing in the richer sort, an uncharitable one to the poorer, a perfect mark of slavery, and nips your commonwealth in the fairest blossom." All classes, indeed, excepting the zemindars, whom the permanent settlement of the Lower Provinces has secured in the possession of the lands, would concur in the propriety of such a regulation; and even to the zemindars themselves, such advantages might be offered as would obtain their consent, without involving any infringement of their proprietory rights.

One plan which suggests itself, is to encourage the zemindars to grant leases, by making a remission in the amount of their land-tax, in proportion to the length of lease granted. If an abatement of one per cent. were granted for leases of ten years and upwards, and of three per cent. for leases in perpetuity; the certainty of immediate profit would probably induce the zemindars to accept the terms; and the farmers and cultivators being secured in the enjoyment of the fruits of their industry, at least for the shorter period, would have a strong interest to exert themselves in improving the condition of their lands. It may indeed be objected, that such a measure would benefit an order of men, the zemindars, who, whatever may have been the case with their predecessors, are now in no want of such assistance; but if, in benefiting the poor classes, this be unavoidable, without a direct violation of acknowledged proprietory rights, it may be remarked, that as the increased amount of rents has, in almost all instances, taken place rather from the extension, than from the improvement, of agriculture—as the same slovenly husbandry that was in use fifty years ago still continues to prevail—there is reason for believing that increase, great as it has been, does not preclude the hope of considerable improvement in the quality and quantity of produce being effected, by the exertion of the cultivators and small farmers, should the encouragement now suggested be afforded them. On the contrary, with the increased circulation of money, which the new order of things would create, and the consequent fall in the rate of interest, the industrious would be able to procure the necessary funds for increasing their stock and produce, without the risk of ruining themselves by the accumulating interest of their outlay, as is the case at present.

And if, in this respect, the Upper Provinces would gain more than the Lower, in proportion to the check to improvement, which cannot but have been the effect of their expectation of receiving a permanent settlement, having so repeatedly been disappointed, this effect of the measure may perhaps be considered as rather an additional recommendation of it, as it will tend to bind those more closely to the soil, who, from their geographical position, are most exposed to external aggression. Rendered comparatively independent in his circumstances, the cultivator would not fail to profit by the example set before him by the European settlers, in procuring for himself the comforts and conveniences of life, and in qualifying himself for taking a share in the affairs of his district and country. The settlers would form a nucleus of intelligence and industry, the presence of which could not fail to have a favourable influence upon the minds, as well as the actions, of the population; mixing with the natives as farmers, planters, and traders, bound to them, in short, by one common interest, and by reciprocal good offices, they would give strength and consistency to the mass in time of peace, and in war they would organize and conduct levies, and perform all the duties of a brave and active yeomanry, sufficient to animate the allegiance of all orders, and place the country in perfect security against external aggression or internal revolt.

Not only would the condition of the native population be greatly improved by the measure proposed, but the state would directly participate in the advantages conferred upon the agricultural classes. The interest of wealthy and intelligent landholders would prompt them to undertake those works of public utility, the expense of which is now defrayed principally by the state, as lord paramount. Local charges of this nature form a large deduction from the gross rents, and, in addition to the cost of management and collection, which, it is to be presumed, would also be diminished, greatly reduce the net receipts of revenue. The redemption of land-tax by some; the reasonable terms on which others would lend their aid in superintending and remitting the collections; and the consequent abolition of various offices, which the present state of the country renders indispensable, would not fail very shortly to relieve the Government from charges, the saving of which would more than compensate for the diminution in the stipulated amount of their land-revenue. The Government, by rigidly adhering to the *principle* of universal proprietorship, has become justly obnoxious to the reproach of having contributed little—nothing towards the embellishment of the country, or the convenience of the inhabitants, generally, by the execution of works of public utility. Indian history is full of descriptions of the magnificent edifices, and other works of art, completed by former sovereigns and provincial rulers. Firoze Shah, we are informed in Dow's translation of Ferishta, built fifty great sluices, forty mosques, thirty schools, twenty caravanserais, a hundred palaces, five hospitals, a hundred tombs, ten baths, ten spires, a hundred and fifty wells, a hundred bridges, &c. &c. Baber, in his Memoirs, tells us that he ordered a minar, or turret, to be raised at every nine coss, and a post-house* at every ten coss, with a relay of six horses; and he is never tired of speaking of the number of gardens and palaces which he erected and planned. Shere Shah, Ackbar, Jehangler, Shah Jehan, and Aurungzebe, appear also to have vied with each other in magnificence of this nature; and the great officers of state, in all parts of the empire, have left behind them monuments of their taste and liberality. The costly materials which they employed, together with the grand scale and mas-

* The quickest mode of travelling now in use, or indeed attainable at present, in Bengal, is by what is called Dawk; that is, by palanquin conveyance, at the rate of about four miles an hour!

sive style of the edifices alluded to, form a remarkable contrast with the small and unpretending buildings erected by the English. Nothing, indeed, can be more striking than the difference between the approach to Delhi, or Agra, even in their present state of decay, and that to Calcutta, after its having been nearly a century the capital of our Eastern empire, the seat of our Government, and the residence of the most opulent of all classes, whether European or native. In the former, the road is lined with the ruins of palaces, gardens, fountains, tanks, serais, baths, in short, et *quicquid tantæ præmittitur urbi*—whilst the latter exhibits nothing from which, at the distance of a mile from the city, the traveller could be led to suppose that he was approaching a place of greater consequence than an ordinary country-town. The reproach which Burke thundered against his countrymen in the East is not yet wiped away; and though, perhaps, it cannot now be said, that "were we to be driven out of India this day, nothing would remain to tell that it had been possessed, during the inglorious period of our dominion, by any thing better than the ouran-outang or the tiger," yet the monuments of state or beneficence left behind us, would be comparatively few indeed; and, excepting in the town of Calcutta itself, they would be almost entirely confined to the repairing of Ali Murdan's and Firoze Shah's canals, the construction of an imperfect military road from the seat of Government to the Upper Provinces, and the erection of a gaol in all the principal towns.

The influence upon the minds of men, which is created by an attention to whatever contributes to adorn the face of the country, and adds to the comfort and convenience of the inhabitants, is at all times sufficiently great to become an object worthy of the consideration of Government. Attachment to the spot on which we were born is not a mere sentiment grounded upon early association, but has for its basis the substantial advantages which that spot affords. To strengthen these claims is to nourish the spirit of patriotism; and a wise government will never relax in its efforts to promote a feeling upon which the safety of the country may eventually depend. In India, especially, all our institutions should have this object in view, in order that a foundation may be laid for organizing an efficient provincial army, and a regular system of defence, in the furtherance of which all ranks of the community may be interested. The diffusion of instruction amongst all classes, together with the encouragement to industry which has just been recommended, will engender a spirit of pride and independence in the peasantry of the country, and render them bold, active, and capable of encountering the fatigues of a soldier's life in time of need. A plan for raising regiments in each district, officered, as much as possible, from the gentry, British, Indo-British, and native,* of the neighbourhood, would not only encourage the feeling of patriotism, and attachment to the soil, amongst the soldiery, but dispose the whole country to take an interest in the events of war, and keep up a salutary emulation and rivalry between the several corps of the army. During peace, such troops as were necessary might be stationed, as much as convenient, in the district where they were raised, and employed in the execution of such works of public utility as would at once furnish them with ample occupation, and conduce to the general advantage of the community.

* Speaking of the Roman conquests, Gibbon remarks, "In their manners and internal policy, the colonies formed a perfect representation of their great parent; and they were soon endeared to the natives by the ties of friendship and alliance. They effectually diffused a reverence for the Roman name, and a desire, which was seldom disappointed, of sharing, in due time, its honours and advantages.—The grandsons of the Gauls, who had besieged Julius Cæsar in Alesia, commanded legions, governed provinces, and were admitted into the Senate of Rome. Their ambition, instead of disturbing the tranquillity of the state, was intimately connected with its safety and greatness."—*Decline and Fall* c. 2.

The pay and subsistence of the army should be sufficient to induce men of good character and abilities to enrol themselves. The honourable poverty, as it is called, in which it is deemed politic to retain the military profession, becomes a mischievous fallacy when carried so far as to lower the defenders of the country in the estimation of their fellow men. If poverty induce contempt in every other class of society, it certainly will not promote in the breast of a soldier, those sentiments upon which his character and intrepidity in a great measure depend. The pay of soldiers should of course be regulated by the rate of wages, generally obtaining, in the country where they are employed; but an individual engaging himself in the profession of arms, should not only be maintained during the continuance of his employment, but he should be recompensed, according to the length of his service, upon rejoining his fellow countrymen, and resuming the habits of life which his enrolment had interrupted. Greater risk is incurred from the effect of military licence, by drawing a distinct line between the soldier and the citizen, than by encouraging them to cherish reciprocal feelings of kindness and confidence, and to entertain a common sympathy for the prosperity of the state. For this purpose, the formation of a regular militia should be encouraged; and, in recruiting for the army, men who have been brought up to regular trades should be preferred. In all situations where active military service was not required of them, they should be employed in the execution of public or private works, according to their several qualifications, upon such additional wages as would be a sufficient compensation for their labour.* Independent of the general advantages attendant upon this system, if steadily adhered to, it is probable that it would materially affect the institution of castes among the natives, by setting a bounty upon useful endowments; instead of filling the ranks, as at present, with men who, in the common phrase, are said to be fit for soldiers because they are fit for nothing else.

Little or no effect, however, from a plan of this

* According to Van Halen, (Narrative, &c.) this seems to be very much the case with the Russian army. The colonel of a regiment is said to be allowed to profit by the industry of his men, when military duty is suspended. "The soldiers then become masons, carpenters, smiths, &c. or engage in whatever occupation they may be hired for; so that, as they are furnished by the colonel with suitable dresses, that their uniforms may not suffer during the time they are thus employed, they cannot be recognised as soldiers, except by their mustachios. Besides, there are always a certain number of men employed in the workshops belonging to the regiment, in every description of trade; consequently, every thing that can possibly be wanted for the corps is made by the soldiers."

nature, can be expected, until measures are adopted for diffusing throughout the country the benefits of elementary instruction in the mechanical arts, agriculture, and manufactures, by the possession of which the people will learn the value of labour, and be able to put forth their strength in the great field of human industry. Many people imagine that this useful measure is in actual operation, in consequence of the forty-third section of the charter of 1813, directing that "a sum of not less than one lac of rupees, (10,000*l.*) shall be annually set apart and applied to the revival and improvement of literature, and the encouragement of the learned natives of India, and for the introduction and promotion of a knowledge of the sciences among the inhabitants of the British territories in India, &c." When, however, it is recollected that British India is supposed to contain nearly ninety millions of inhabitants, it will not be deemed surprising that the expenditure of such a small sum as ten thousand pounds is found totally inadequate to the production of any visible effect upon the manners and habits of the people. The Hindoo and Mohammedan Colleges, established in Calcutta, are undoubtedly useful institutions, as far as the learned natives of India are concerned; and while some of the former bid fair to spread a knowledge of the English language among the natives of the higher classes of Calcutta, the latter is chiefly instrumental in qualifying Mohammedans for the appointments of vakeels, or pleaders in the law courts. The gradual introduction of the English language, however, is a point of so much importance, that any institution, which has for its object the perpetuation of the existing absurdities of a body of law administered in a language alike foreign (and generally unknown) to the judge who presides, as well as to the suitors and witnesses, cannot but be considered as a misappropriation of the funds in question. If the English language were made an indispensable qualification * for

* Of late years, a great deal too much importance has been attached to the acquisition of the languages of the country, as a qualification for office. Sir John Malcolm very justly observes, that strict principle, general knowledge, and sound judgment, should constitute the principal considerations in estimating the character of a public servant. "As an auxiliary," he adds, "to the developement and useful action of these qualities, an acquaintance with the languages of India is most desirable; but unassociated with them, it is nothing, and injury has sometimes resulted to the public from a too exclusive consideration being given to this attainment."—*Pol. Hist*. vol. ii. p. 187. It may be questioned, indeed, whether a nation was ever civilized by its conquerors making themselves masters of its language. The study of a language, almost necessarily induces an imitation of the trains of thought, and even of the manners, the traces of which it has been em-

every public employment, it would tend, more than any thing else, to the encouragement of general knowledge, and, as a natural consequence, to the gradual weaning of the minds of the natives, from the absurd superstition by which their ener-

ployed to record; and the acquisition of a living language in particular, is not more aided by a quickness of ear and comprehension, than by a certain mimic inflection of voice and gesture. The truth of this remark is so generally felt, that most persons, in their first colloquial attempt in a foreign tongue, run into the extreme of action and grimace, in order the more readily to make themselves understood. But if this be the case with a mere accomplishment, how much more true it must be, where the language in question is that by the aid of which the greater part of our official business, as well as familiar intercourse with those around us, is carried on. Perhaps there are few causes which have had a more direct tendency to retard the progress of European arts and civilization in the East, than the general favour which Oriental studies have found in the eyes of our countrymen; and certain it is, that many instances are to be found of promising talent for the public service having degenerated into mere pedantry from the same cause. There are, accordingly, few Oriental scholars in India who have distinguished themselves in other branches of learning or speculation, or who have established a reputation as men of enlarged views, even on subjects connected with their pursuits. They mostly evince a sort of literary proselytism, and are occupied only in upholding the credit of their adopted faith. Some brilliant exceptions there undoubtedly are, and perhaps no one shines more conspicuously as such than the writer already referred

gies are clogged, and which sits like an incubus upon both their mental and physical powers. A knowledge of the English language would, in this sense, conduce both to the moral and physical advantage of the natives, and would shortly render

to in the note; owing, probably, to his active employment and varied occupations having so absorbed his attention, as to have prevented his penetrating too deeply into the wilderness of Eastern lore. But this pre-eminence, as it is highly honourable to him as a man of talent, only renders it the more to be regretted, that he should have expressed opinions so adverse to the general improvement of the natives of India, and so little in accordance with that spirit which might be expected from an independent Briton, who owed his own early rise to the display of considerable ability, and to the exertion of a frankness and uprightness of character, not only highly creditable to himself, but capable of producing the best effects upon the condition of those who, more perhaps than any race on earth, need the advocacy of commanding talent, in unison with powerful influence. What was said by a French writer, on the conversion of Abubekre by Mahomet, may, with a little alteration, be applied to Sir John Malcolm. "When a man of consequence falls into an error, the contagion spreads with rapidity. The vulgar appreciate the value of an opinion according to the idea which they form of the merit of those who embrace it; and they imagine, that where the head is sound, the heart cannot err." But whether the opinions which that writer has lately put forth on the subject of a maximum taxation on land, the necessity for absolute government, and the slavery of the press in India, proceed from his head or his heart, they are equally to be regretted.

them fit to take a share in conducting the affairs of the country, which their utter ignorance now affords an excuse for depriving them of. Education would not only engender new tastes and new wants, but confer the means of gratifying them. A thousand channels of industry would be opened, and doubtless new forms of invention would be "bodied forth," which it is impossible, under present circumstances, to foretell; for, as there are stars, the light of which astronomers tell us has not even yet had time to reach the sphere which we inhabit, so there are combinations of thought in the fertile mind of man which it is hardly possible to imagine. In proportion as the genius of the natives was called forth, the increased intercourse with Europeans, which would be the direct consequence of their newly-acquired intelligence, would elevate their moral character, and imbue them with a spirit which could not but be favourable to the propagation of the religion of the Gospel amongst them. It would, indeed, be doing no less injustice to the purity of that religion, than to the dignity of human nature, to suppose that any thing but utter ignorance could retain the natives of India in the gross system of idolatry by which they are now debased; and the evident feeling of shame that is perceptible in the countenance of every native above the ordinary stamp, when the ceremonials of his religion are spoken of in his presence, should be hailed as a good omen of the ultimate effect which the diffusion of knowledge will produce. It is easy to conceive how the most gifted genius, when standing alone and unsupported amidst a priest-ridden population, and having none but repulsive and haughty Europeans, in high official stations, to resort to, will cling to the errors of the religion in which he was brought up, even in spite of his better reason; but when the number of those with whom he can indulge in a community of thought is increased, there will be no longer any such reason for concealment; and conversion* will rapidly proceed, as

* The danger of exciting insurrection on the score of religion, where we are so vastly outnumbered by our native subjects, and of rousing opposition on the only point on which our native army is likely to make common cause against us with their fellow-countrymen, is too obvious to be insisted on: it is impossible, therefore, not to agree with Sir John Malcolm (*Pol. Hist.* vol. ii. p. 265.) in his general reasoning on this subject; but when he asserts that the progress of the British was accelerated by their adoption of this principle, and that of the Portuguese and French impeded by neglecting it, neither history nor reason will bear him out. If the Portuguese had surrounded their settlements and towns with native Christians, they would at least have been certain of the allegiance of their subjects; and their fall would have been retarded, instead of hastened, in proportion to the number of adherents which religion had procured

it always should do, by the light of reason and reflection:—*non est religionis cogere religionem*—but example and education are at all times legitimate means of producing conviction.

With the slender means, however, at present at the disposal of Government, it is unreasonable to expect that any decisive improvement, of the kind alluded to, will be effected. In Calcutta, the success of several public and private establish-

them. They would, in short, have been less dependent on Europe for recruiting their strength. It was, however, the decline of their power and influençe in Europe, and the consequent want of support from the mother-country, added to the active and persevering hostility of the Dutch, that occasioned their downfall in the East; and these causes were quite sufficient, notwithstanding the assistance which they might have derived from a Christian population, even had it been as numerous as the writer would persuade us. In like manner, the French were overmatched by the English having been enabled, in consequence of their possessing the command of the ocean, to intercept all supplies in time of war; and in consequence, too, of their growing wealth and influence with the natives giving them political ascendency at the several native courts. Religion had no influence in this case; and if, in the time of Dupleix and Lally, the religious feelings of the Mohammedans and Hindoos were outraged, the historian, in order to demonstrate the truth of his position, should have given us some proofs of positive injury to the French interests from the cause. It is, indeed, so little certain that the Mohammedans would evince any interest in a professed intention to convert the Hindoos by priests, or,

ments, but particularly of the Anglo-Indian College, has led many to form an exaggerated estimate of the measures now in operation, and of the general encouragement given by Government, as well as individuals, for promoting instruction throughout the country. Those at Calcutta are chiefly supported by the exertions of private individuals; and the countenance afforded by Govern-

*vice versa*, that the latter would trouble themselves in behalf of the former, that many people believe we might with perfect safety make use of one sect to coerce the other, did not our ideas of toleration and religious freedom forbid the deed. The association of a war of religion with every tumult in which the Mohammedans are concerned, arises out of the mistake of assuming that their green flag is a rallying point in cases of this nature exclusively; whereas it is their national standard on all occasions, and is hoisted to collect Mohammedans, just as the Union Jack serves as a signal for Englishmen. It may, perhaps, be true, that the English evinced less solicitude for the propagation of the Christian faith, than any other adventurers; trade and conquest, indeed, appear to have absorbed all their attention; but to assert that they purposely avoided what the historian is pleased to call the "great errors" of their rivals, is to say they acted upon principle throughout, and to take credit for their sins of omission, as well as those of commission. A total want of principle, other than a constant readiness to aggrandize themselves where they had power to do so, is the most remarkable characteristic of the early progress made by the English in India.

ment is generally supposed to be almost entirely attributable to the influence of some leading members of the society; whilst native gentlemen of rank and wealth, though many of them undoubtedly men of liberal and enlightened minds, are not insensible to the vanity of seeing their names associated with those of the magnates of the realm in this or any other public undertaking. Certain it is, that at a distance from the capital, the spectacle of a native of rank interesting himself in the education of his countrymen, is, if not entirely unknown, at least very rare; and from this circumstance, together with the small number, and comparatively short residence of the missionaries and others, on whom the practical charge of the schools devolves, no perceptible progress has been made, or can be expected, in a work requiring so much persevering attention, and so steady an adherence to system, as the progressive reform which it is desirable to effect in the habits and manners of the population of Hindostan. Without the aid of a body of men who, from being settled in the country, will be impelled as much by a feeling of mutual convenience and advantage, as by a sense of their duty as Christians, to attend to the improvement of those around them, no lasting impression will be made

—our utmost efforts, like writing on the sand, will be liable to be effaced by every change, even to the slightest ruffling on the surface.

In every point of view, then, is Colonization the only effectual remedy—the "one thing needful" for the salvation of Hindostan; whether we look to augmenting the efficiency of the civil Government, and enabling it to fulfil the duties to which it is now confessedly inadequate, without an addition to its expenditure which the revenue of the country could never support; or to the defence of the country against foreign invasion, without rendering it onerous, out of all proportion, to the mother country; or, lastly, to the improvement and well-being of the subject-millions committed to our sway, and the eventual establishment of Christianity over some of the fairest portion of the habitable globe.

THE END.